Praise for *God's Song*

Keys to Finding Joy in the Midst of Difficulties – A Devotional Journey

"Susan Berg Heeg's life is a chronicle of God's faithful one. As I read these pages, time and time again I found myself encouraged, cheered, and uplifted by these vignettes of God's gracious presence – something we all could use in greater abundance."

Jeff Gissing
– Director of Bible Acquisitions,
Tyndale House Publishing

"Susan Berg Heeg's *God's Song in Your Soul* is an insightful look at how the songs of the faith can inspire and calm our souls when we are experiencing pain, turmoil, fear, and doubt. In it, she shares through her own experiences, the joy that you can find when you completely trust God, even in the deepest depth of despair. Each "song" helps us understand a characteristic of God that will help us not only through our own experience, but also give us insights into some of the many attributes of our God. At the end of each "song" is a helpful key to finding joy. In each key, Susan asks us questions about our own experiences with that particular song, and she challenges us to take a few moments to reflect and share what those thoughts are. Has life been a little bit difficult lately? Does it seem as if God isn't there for you? Do you feel abandoned by Him at times? If so, you are in need of joy. And the good news is you can find joy even amid pain and despair. God has songs for your soul. Allow Susan to help you discover them."

Pastor Dennis Cocks
New Hope Baptist Church, Plano, IL

"Susan Berg Heeg's devotional journey, *God's Song in Your Soul*, is nothing short of a gem. I have been encouraged to the core by how God is with us through our highs and lows and how our story can be a blessing to the body of believers. So often we think that we have no story to tell. What have I experienced that I could pass on or share with others? What do I have to offer? I am not clever enough, good or sinless enough, Christian enough, educated enough, charismatic or extroverted enough. Who am I? Well, reading Susan's book, we realize we're in good company, and we also realize that it is not truly about us; it's about God. We might not always know what to do, but we know who does; we know *Him*! I love how apparent Susan makes that from her own life and walk with God, and I love how practical she makes it for us to reflect on our own lives at the end of each chapter. I also constantly found myself thinking of young people I work with as I was reading and am truly looking forward to giving them this book."

Bjørne-Inge Aurdal
– Young Adult Pastor and
Missionary in Reykjavik, Iceland

"In *God's Song in Your Soul*, Susan Berg Heeg shares her story... but a story to which most of us can relate. How her life was like a house that weathered many storms, some that were self-induced and those that came up out of nowhere. However, the house kept standing, because it was on a firm foundation. In her devotional journey, she shares how God's word and music were the constants in which she was able to find peace, hope, love, strength, and joy to continue the journey. In every storm, there is an invitation for the reader to pause, reflect, and welcome the change that your life is facing. Storms will be hard. So, whatever love for God is in your heart... nurture it. Develop it. Grow it. Spread it and strengthen your foundation. Susan's book provides the opportunity to do that."

Pastor Andy Morgan
Former Founding Pastor of River Valley
Community Church, Aurora, IL

GOD'S SONG IN YOUR SOUL

Keys to Finding Joy in the Midst of Difficulties

A Devotional Journey

Susan Berg Heeg

Interior Formatting by Oseyi Okoeguale (ose_solutions)

Book Cover Design by Rehmanx

ISBN# 979-8-9864964-1-2

In memory of my parents, Cecile and Donald Berg, who taught me about God. They showed me what having God's song in their hearts looked like whether in happy or difficult times. They loved me unconditionally through all of my ups and downs. They were full of true joy in God and therefore were a great joy in my life! Mom and Dad will always have my love! I can't wait to see them again in Heaven!

My parents, Cecile and Donald Berg, are joyful in Salzburg, Austria at the Gazebo from *The Sound of Music*.

Dedicated to my best friend and "sister", Barbara Gibson Neely, who has been there for me for 54 years through my struggles and the miracles in my life. Always questioning, always faithful, always thinking through life's events. Barb has challenged me to look to God for answers and never settle for the status quo in my relationship with God. As a musician and choir director in church, she has also helped to bring the hymns of God's song to my heart! When it comes to a friend standing with you no matter what happens throughout your life, Barb has been God's person for me. I love you, Barb!

I am with Barb at a picnic in our early days as Christians.

Acknowledgments

I would like to thank the following people:

David Heeg, my dear husband, has taken on many extra chores around the house, loved me, and made me laugh over the years. These gifts also allowed me to finish the book to which God has led me. You are greatly loved, David! You are always my rock! God really blessed me with you!

My wonderful stepsons, Jason Heeg Sr. (Mish, his wife) and David Heeg Jr. (Andrea, his wife), have lived through the last forty years of my journey and have loved and supported me all the way. We are truly family. I am thankful!

My awesome grandchildren, Kathryn Heeg, David Heeg III, Andrew Heeg, Jason Heeg Jr., Anthony Heeg, and Emma Heeg, have given me love and laughs over the years. They have encouraged me in my writing. Thank you for your love and also for being so good to my mom, Grandma Cec, in her final time with us. I love you all! My prayers for you will be written in Heaven.

Mom and Dad raised me to be a Christian and were patient and understanding of my ups and downs. Their prayers for me are written in Heaven.. their new home. I am forever grateful!

My brother, Jim, was my best friend as we grew up.. moving and adjusting to different locations over the years. I am thankful and will always love him and his family!

My half-brother, Darryl, was a great help in my writing of my chapter on God's gift of finding him after 70 years of being apart. Thank you, Darryl, for your kindness and love.

Barb Gibson Neely, my best longtime friend, has been beside me throughout my journey to find joy in the midst of difficulties. Thank you for thinking to invite me to the Spiritual Autobiography Zoom class through your church in 2020. Thank you for always being there for me!

Pastor Emily Davis, First Congregational Church, Crystal Lake, IL, offered a Spiritual Autobiography Zoom Class, which started me on the path to writing this book, and she also did a very thorough edit of the book draft. Thank you, Emily!

My Accomplished Authors Zoom teacher, Sue Sundstrom, deserves high awards for helping me focus on what God would want to be included in the book and for teaching and encouraging me to finish my book and get it published. She has a God-given gift! What a wonderful teacher and friend!

Nicole Roth, Louise Campion, Teri, Rose, Lauri, Coetta, Cheri, and all the women and men who have been in the Accomplished Authors Group have supported me and prayed for me along the way. I am thankful!

Huntley Brown, the famous pianist for the Billy Graham Organization who played at Reverend Graham's funeral, allowed me to use an example from a wonderful sermon he gave at our church, Westminster Presbyterian, in Aurora, IL. Thank you, Huntley!

Retired Lutheran Bishop and old friend, Wayne Miller, allowed me to use a quote from his Facebook post. So appreciated, Wayne!

A friend of mine from college, Jay Newman, is the administrator of a private but open to others group on Facebook called "Positivity Power". He allowed me to use a quote from his post in the group. Thank you, Jay!

Allie McLarty allowed me to share her story from her third-grade year with me. What encouragement you and your mom gave me in my teaching! Thank you!

Melissa Carter, a former third grader in 1971, allowed me to share the tragic story of her son's death. God be with you, Melissa! You are loved!

I thank Sue Ochsenschlager and Liz Bosworth for praying for my mom and for allowing me to use a story in this book that included them.

Jeff Gissing, Pastor Dennis Cocks, Pastor Andy Morgan, and Bjørne-Inge Aurdal (a Christian missionary for young adults in Iceland) have my gratitude for reading my book without knowing my personal background well and giving me feedback on the ideas, format, and God's truth.

Many pastors have taught me, and friends and relatives have prayed for me as I have focused on what God would want to convey in this book. I especially thank Sonia Foster, Carolyn Hansen, Sue Anderson, Liz Selander, Gayle Nelson, Sharon

Hughes, Cathy Cocks, LaVerne Taylor, Gwen Morgan, Linda Dudley, Bev Aieta, Mickie O'Donnell, Carol Michels, Beverly Gonzalez, and Claire Pepper. I have such gratitude to all of the members of the Westminster Presbyterian Church of Aurora, IL Women's Bible Study and Martha Circle for taking a very active part in encouraging and praying for me. You are all blessings in my life!

Renée Bill, a member of the Billy Graham Evangelistic Association Legal Department, helped me to hunt down book references for quotes from Billy Graham which I used in my book. I am so thankful for her hard work and kindness in the process.

Mike Mishler of Lincat Photography in Holly, MI has given his time and talent freely to give me the right to use a picture he had placed on the Great Lakes Military Cemetery website. I wanted to use the picture on my website and in the book. Thank you, Mike!

I would finally like to thank Barry "Angel", who cared enough to follow the leading of the Holy Spirit to stand on a street corner and show me the reality and the love of God.

Table of Contents

Introduction

A Song of God's Songs

I froze... horrified by the sight before me. There she was, my 93-year-old mom fighting and yelling at nurses, blood spurting everywhere as she tugged at the IV and monitors. Since calling me earlier, nurses were scrambling to fix what Mom was destroying. Another nurse heroically held her newly replaced hip steady. It was 4 in the morning, and Mom was screaming that she was in prison. She was going to get the ropes off herself and get out of there.

The nurse holding Mom's hip said, "Cecile, Susan is here."

"She is?" Mom asked. "Please help me, Susan! Don't you see they've tied me up?"

I stepped to her side. "You have to calm down now, Mom. You had surgery and have to let the nurses take care of you."

After my numerous attempts to reach her, Mom shouted, "No! You can't be my Susan. You're an imposter! My Susan wouldn't leave me in this prison!!"

I didn't know what to do for this dear woman whom I loved with all of my heart. She thought I was an imposter! The nurses were telling me that Mom had a bad reaction to the anesthesia. When she wouldn't listen to me, I cried.

I began to pray and knew what to do. Singing quietly, all of Mom's favorite hymns poured from my heart.

"Abide with me, fast falls the eventide. The darkness deepens, Lord, with me abide. When other helpers fail and comforts flee, help of the helpless, O abide with me."[1]

Mom's eyes closed.

"Great is Thy faithfulness. Great is Thy faithfulness. Morning by morning new mercies I see. All I have needed, Thy hand hath provided. Great is Thy faithfulness, Lord unto me."[2]

Her breathing slowed.

"I come to the Garden alone when the dew is still on the roses... And He walks with me and He talks with me. And He tells me I am His own. And the joy we share as we tarry there, none other has ever known."[3]

With each song, she seemed to be quieting and listening. Praying that the Holy Spirit was working in Mom's soul, I was holding her hand. I finished singing "Oh How He Loves You and Me"[4] just for Mom including her name and mine. How God loves my mom!

There was silence... Then looking at me peacefully with clear eyes, she said, "Susan, that was beautiful!" Mom was back.

～～～～～～～～～～～～～～～～～～

This was not the first time that God had carried me through a tough situation and not the last. Are you struggling with fear or doubt in the Lord as you are going through the difficult times of your life? Do you sometimes wonder if God is there with you? I have had those

[1] Lyte, Henry (Words), Copyright © 1847, William Monk (Music), Copyright © 1861, "Abide with Me", in the Public Domain.
[2] Chisholm, Thomas Obediah (Words), William Marion Runyan (Music), Copyright © 1923, "Great Is Thy Faithfulness", in the Public Domain.
[3] Miles, Charles Austin, Copyright © 1912, "In the Garden", in the Public Domain.
[4] Kaiser, Kurt, Copyright © 1975, "Oh How He Loves You and Me", Los Angeles, California: Word Music, Inc.

thoughts. In this book, I will share my journey to find the joy of the Lord - even in the tough times. Perhaps your life has many blessings, but you haven't realized the full joy that knowing Jesus can bring. As human beings, when all is going right, we sometimes don't reach out to God as much as we do in hard times. Joy is not simply happiness. It is not a feeling. What is joy in the Lord? It is knowledge in your heart. It is peace and confidence that God is with you and in control no matter what you are going through in life. God's song deep in your soul is the joy and peace you find when you know the Lord in good or bad times.

Music has always been an important part of my life. As I encountered times in my life, or as I wrote about them in this book, a hymn would come to my mind. Portions of these hymns have been included with life lessons. Singing praise to God can bring you joy.

As I write this book, I am constantly aware that I am telling my own story. Will it be too much of me? Will it not be pointing to God? It is something I pray about each day that I write. I want you to know that I am sharing my journey and the love of the Lord God, because I love you. I pray each day that you will not hear "preaching" from me. This is God's story of what He has done.

It has not been a straight line to realizing this joy that God can give. There have been questions, pain, and hard lessons along my way. I would never tell you that I have all the answers. Knowing God and learning is an ongoing process. God has simply put it on my heart to share my experiences and point to the One God who was with me throughout them. You may have known the Lord Jesus for years. You may have gone to church but haven't thought very deeply about God. Maybe you don't truly know and depend on God. Whatever has happened in your life and whatever may happen in the future, God is there. I am sharing twenty-eight of God's keys to a life of joy

3

- grace and love and the peace of God. HE ALONE has brought me through these events and has also given me a life of blessings.

The difficulties of life can bring you many types of pain - grief, physical, emotional, or spiritual pain. Are you ready to find joy in the midst of your difficulties? After sharing a portion of my journey, I will discuss how it may apply to you. Then, at the end of each chapter, I will share a key to finding joy in the midst of difficulties. I also give you a chance to think about God's mercies in your life. Not all of the questions will apply to you. Take what strikes you and let God work in your heart and thoughts. Pray and reflect upon what God has done in your life. My prayer for you as you read these "songs" is that you will open your heart and mind to the character of God, his awesome power, and his song for you. As the Bible says:

> You will go out in joy and be led forth in peace; The mountains and hills will burst into song before you, and all the trees of the field will clap their hands... This will be for the Lord's renown, for an everlasting sign, that will endure forever.
>
> **Isaiah 55:12-13 (NIV)**

A Song of God's Nurturing Love

Though he giveth or he taketh, God his children
ne'er forsaketh. His loving purpose solely to
preserve them safe and holy.
- Caroline W. Sandell Berg

ooking out the bus window, I could see nothing but the rain streaming down. How could it be that I was on my way to a funeral? My mind struggled to grasp the situation at hand. I was a freshman at Augustana College in Rock Island, IL and had received a phone call. My first love from high school had died - killed in an automobile accident. Tears running down my cheeks like the rain, I couldn't believe this was real.

Arriving at the church for the visitation and funeral service, I quietly grabbed a seat in the back of the sanctuary. It was all I could do to make myself go up to the casket. It was almost more than I could bear. This body, now lifeless, had been so animated and full of laughter. Joking and teasing and alive - that's what it should have been. Not this!

Al and I met during my sophomore year of high school in Rochester, Illinois, a small farming community outside of the Illinois state capital, Springfield. Al was a year older, and it was at a choir party when we sat together. We simply had fun, and he made me laugh harder than I had ever laughed. I was smitten. On the day of his funeral, thoughts of dating during high school were floating through my memory. I remembered our first kiss - my first ever sweet kiss. How could this be? How could God have allowed this young man of his to be killed so soon in life?

There was an agonizing ongoing ache in my heart.

Questions would haunt me for the rest of my days in college. Back in my bed at Augustana in the dark, thoughts would come each night. *God, why would you do this? Did you do this? Did you allow it? Is there even a God? Are you there, God? Is there really a heaven? Who am I in this universe? Am I but a speck on the Earth, just living out my time here? Is there no meaning to life? Am I real? There must not be a God.* It didn't help that *Time* magazine had come out with a cover that said, "Is God Dead?"[5]. I questioned whether God had ever been there.

My four years of college are a blur. I belonged to a sorority of dear friends, and yet I did not fully participate with them. I dated, but I was afraid to develop any deep type of relationship. In the summers during college, I dated Dave who was a Christian. We had many long talks during which he tried to console me and help me to understand loss and my questions about God. I was not ready to hear him. I got through my classes at Augustana but could have learned more. I seemed to have a difficult time concentrating on anything.

I was raised as a Christian. My loving parents were faithful followers of Jesus who prayed, read the Bible, and modeled care for others in their everyday lives. I sang in the children's choir, and I

---

[5] *Time. The Weekly Magazine*, Copyright © April 8, 1966, Vol. 87 No. 14 Cover Page, New York City: Time Inc. (1966).

even had a solo when we sang *Children of the Heavenly Father*. My solo verse was:

> *Neither life nor death shall ever, from the Lord his children sever.*
> *Unto them his grace he showeth, and their sorrows all he knoweth.*[6]

I joined the marionette club at church in 5th grade where we made our own marionettes and performed Bible stories for the church. Great fun!

After attending Lutheran confirmation classes, I was confirmed in my faith in 8th grade. However, I think I was living and thinking on the surface of myself. I knew specifics of the Bible and the Christian life in general, but I'm not sure I knew them in my heart. I was being a Christian for others - my dear mom and dad and my pastor - but was I believing for me? I guess that was what confirmation was supposed to be all about when you agreed with the teachings of the church and confessed belief in God. However, Al's tragic death made me take a deep dive into my inner self. It was scary and uncertain in there, and I decided it was easier to live outside of myself. A shell hardened around my heart.

After my college graduation, I accepted an elementary teaching position in Aurora, Illinois about forty miles west of Chicago. It was the furthest suburb out, and we had cornfields next to our school. I was dating Marshall, another Augustana graduate. He had been on the football team in college, and I had always had a little crush on him. Marshall lived in beautiful Rock Island along the Mississippi River where Augustana College was located. He was home to see his parents in the Chicago area often, or I went to Rock Island to see

---

[6] Berg, Caroline W. Sandell, (Words), Copyright © 1855, "Children of the Heavenly Father", in the Public Domain.

him. We were trying long-distance dating. Marshall was kind and very good to me, and I thought a relationship was beginning to blossom.

At Christmas time, I was a bridesmaid at the wedding of my best friend, Alison, from Rochester, IL. I attended with my parents. We had a great time and had just walked into my apartment in Wheaton, IL. The phone was ringing. "Hello?" Everything seemed to go in slow motion as I heard a friend's voice on the other end of the phone. My mind and body went limp as I dropped the phone. Marshall died in an automobile accident!

I numbly walked through this funeral. Members of the Augustana football team were pallbearers. Friends from college were there, but many did not even know that Marshall and I had been dating. I was just another college friend at this dear man's funeral. My heart ached from the pain. I just wanted to go to sleep and have the pain gone.

Once more, faced with the finality of death, the questions came again. The shell I had created was now broken and thoughts were flooding my head and heart. Where was the nurturing God of my childhood? Now I wanted to shake my fist at God. *Do you exist at all, God?! Why? Why Al and Marshall? Why me? How could a loving God let this happen to Al and Marshall? Where is God in all of this?!*

~~~~~~~~~~~~~~~~~~~~~~~~~~~~~~~

LET'S TALK ABOUT GOD'S NURTURING LOVE:

You too may have asked yourself at some point in your life... *Where is God in all of this?* Tragedy and loss had brought me to the point of asking many questions of God. I had been to church all of my life. I had learned the lessons from Sunday School that many of you have learned in your lives. I could recite from memory the 66 books of the Bible, and I had learned all the popular Bible verses such as:

> For God so loved the world that He gave His one and only son, that whoever believes in Him shall not perish but have eternal life. For God did not send His son into the world to condemn the world, but to save the world through Him.
>
> **John 3:16–17 (NIV)**

God doesn't expect us to be spiritual robots, just taking as truth whatever is taught to us in church. We begin with spiritual baby food in our early lives with God in the form of simple stories from the Bible such as Noah and the animals walking to the ark two by two. This is the point where some Christians stop. They only know the simple stories from childhood. But our loving God wants to nurture us with love and see us grow.

I believe I began to grow at this time because I did express my thoughts to God. I talked with him, and I questioned him. He expects us to examine the scriptures, examine our hearts, talk to him, and ask questions. Without that process, we may have accepted Jesus as our Savior but has he become our Lord? As Lord, God has the key place in our lives. When Jesus is our Lord, we come to him with all of our hurts and questions. Our nurturing loving Lord wants to teach his children. God loves us and sees us through our learning process about him. Even though I have grown in God's knowledge and truth since this very sad part of my life, I continue to have the question – *Why Al and Marshall?* I know a tiny part of the answer. Tough things happen in life. God did not cause these deaths. There is no easy way to accept deaths, but these brought me to a point of being willing to question God and talk to him. That was good. I will not get a full answer until I meet Jesus in Heaven.

KEY TO FINDING GOD'S JOY #1:

Ask questions about and to God. Without diving deeply into the questions that we encounter as we travel through this life, we will have a shallow faith. Do not be satisfied with spiritual baby food or just walk away figuring that it is too hard to find answers. God continues to want to lovingly nurture you. When you are nurtured, you grow. Pray. Look to the Bible scriptures for answers. Talk to people of faith about the answers. Not all questions can indeed be easily answered, but don't be afraid to ask. Acknowledge the pain which you have. Inside of that pain, you will lean into God receiving his peace and joy deep down in your heart when you seek, whether or not you find the answer. One day, when you know and meet God in Heaven, you will learn the answer.

PRAYERFULLY THINK ABOUT YOUR OWN LIFE WITH GOD:

Have you gone to church all of your life as I did, but you don't think much about God during the week? Do you think that maybe there is something you are missing? Is there a difficult time that is in your life which has left you asking, "How could a loving God let this happen?" What is that? Do you ever lay in bed, trying to work through the deep questions of life? What questions do you ask in bed? Do you ever doubt and just about reject God? What is happening in your life to make you doubt? What questions do you have about God? He wants you to think about him in a life-changing way.. to nurture you. He knows your thoughts before you know them. Take an opportunity here to reflect on these questions I have asked. Remember, you can answer them all or pick and choose. Perhaps you would like to take this time to write down some questions you still have for God.

_____

_____

_____

_____

_____

_____

_____

_____

_____

_____

_____

_____

_____

_____

_____

_____

_____

_____

_____

_____

_____

_____

A Song of
God's Patience

The Spirit pleads for life's devotion to its goal.
- Menno Simons and James H. Rogers

During this time after Al and Marshall's deaths, I was confused and lonely. My long-time friend from college and apartment roommate, Barb, was my best friend. Through her, I could always count on an analytical view of life. She seemed to be able to see the big picture but analyze the parts of a situation as well. Barb was a beautiful red-headed junior high teacher, and her temperament was mild and soothing. I could count on her to talk about anything in life. However, Barb was quite socially booked. After spending many nights alone at home, I was depressed.

One night I decided to get out of the apartment and go to a bar by myself just to be near people. Sitting on a barstool amid the crowd, I didn't want to dance or talk to anyone. However, this man came to sit next to me, made me giggle, and I took a step into the abyss. I drove him to his home that night, where the smell of stale marijuana and incense floated in the air. Danny was a drug dealer. This straight-laced schoolteacher was in a situation way over her head, and I didn't even seem to realize it or care as we began dating.

I didn't use the drugs. Danny seemed to like that about me. Matter of fact, I think he liked that I was a Christian and was different from other women he had known. What did I like about Danny? At first, I think I was so lonely that I enjoyed that someone was paying attention to me. He was also funny. One time, he took me to his parents' home to proudly introduce me. I was special to him. There was a very vulnerable seeking man hidden under those crazy drugs. To me, he was a person whom I could care for and perhaps help to turn around his life.

At one time I was driving, and he asked to stop at someone's house. He ran in and out quickly. After leaving that house and turning onto a highway, the siren and red lights shown behind me. I pulled over to the side of the road. The police checked my ID and said something about a turn signal. We went on our way.

Later in the week, the phone rang. "This is the FBI. Am I talking with Susan Berg?" When I answered in the affirmative he said, "We would like to know how you know Danny." Shock set in. I was talking to someone from the FBI! I thought back to the traffic stop that week and now assumed that they were surveilling Danny. Perhaps in that traffic stop, they had wondered who on earth I was. Now they knew and were calling me. After some discussion, the FBI agent on the other end of the phone kindly gave me a heads up. "Do you realize how much trouble you could be in if there was a raid at Danny's home when you are there?" Now finally, my trouble started to sink into my head. The FBI shook me to the core.

I spoke to Danny later that day. I did not tell him about the call from the FBI. Perhaps sensing that someone was on his trail, he said, "Can I come and stay at your apartment to kick my heroin habit? I have Methadone to ease the withdrawal."

He probably had a feeling that his home was a dangerous place to be. I cared about him and actually considered helping him. When my roommate, Barb, told her mom about the possibility of Danny coming to our apartment, her mom stepped into the situation. Barb had to move out and leave me if I was to help Danny. He needed professional help to kick a heroin problem. I broke off my relationship with Danny.

Now a flood of questions really came down on me. *How could I have gotten myself into this situation after the way I was raised? Was I not living in reality? Did I have a brain freeze? Maybe the God I thought I knew wasn't there. Did I not believe in Jesus anymore?* This was the greatest break I had in my Christianity. I did not trust my thinking anymore.

Wheaton, IL where I was living with Barb is a quaint town west of Chicago and the home of Wheaton College. Evangelist Billy Graham had attended there, and the Billy Graham Association was located there. It has always been a haven of Christianity. I heard of a bookstore in north Wheaton which had books on many different religions.. even satanism. Seeking truth and peace in my mind, I drove to the bookstore. I explored many of the books on different religions. Nothing seemed to ring true. I knew the God of the Bible. He was there.. but where? I knew in my heart that God had put it in that FBI agent's heart to warn me about the dangers in which I found myself. God was patient with me. He was leading me.. step by step. The very old hymn comes into my heart.

> *O God, thy patience moves my soul to see in Thee the way of life.*
> *Thy purpose an unfolding scroll; Of changes all with meaning rife.*[7]

God was with me and patient in my confusion.

---

[7] Simons, Menno (1496-1561) (Words) Copyright Date Unknown, "O God, They Patience Moves My Soul", in the Public Domain, and James H. Rogers (Music), Copyright © 1914, "Patience, LMD", in the Public Domain.

LET'S TALK ABOUT GOD'S PATIENCE:

Yes. As we proceed through life in our faith, God's lessons for us are like an unfolding scroll. There are changes we encounter. There are questions that we face. There is hardship, and then there are mistakes that one makes when you are not depending on God. You would rather depend on yourself to get you through the hard times of life. We, as Christians, know that we sin when we do not depend on God. We cannot possibly live up to his glory.

> for all have sinned and fall short of the glory of God, and all are justified freely by his grace through the redemption that came by Christ Jesus.
>
> **Romans 3:23 (NIV)**

Was there much joy in this time of my life? No. I did not feel it. I had fallen away from the God I knew. I didn't even realize at this point that there was a way to feel joy in the midst of pain. But God was beginning to show me His ways. He was so patient with me.

You may be saying to yourself, *"I'm a good person. I certainly haven't had any experiences like you did, Susan. I give to the poor, I care about others, and I do my best to be a good citizen. I go to church. I don't sin."* Have you ever been jealous, selfish, greedy, arrogant, or hurtful to others? You have therefore sinned or done wrong to your fellow man and God. So have all of us.

A final note for those of us who have grown up in the church, but we don't see the relevance of Jesus as Lord in our lives anymore. We may not go to church anymore. Let me be clear. The church is NOT a building. It is the body of believers who truly put their faith in God. For some of us, our faith has waned. What is taking the place of Jesus if he is not relevant? Earning money, sleeping in on

Sundays, being able to do whatever we please maybe including that which we know is wrong? Or perhaps many good things like spending time with family, getting exercise, helping out someone else, etc. have become your relevant god. Jesus loves you just as you are. However, deep in your heart, do you have that God-shaped space that is missing something? Deep down, don't you feel that you are missing God's song in your soul? Tough times will come. Will those activities you find relevant help you in the darkest times of your life? Jesus is waiting patiently for you to come back to him.

> Trust in the Lord with all your heart and lean not on your own understanding; in all your ways submit to Him, and he will make your paths straight.
>
> **Proverbs 3:5-6 (NIV)**

KEY TO FINDING GOD'S JOY #2:

Be thankful for the patient God you serve. He knows you. He knows your name. He is with you and forgives you as you make mistakes. God is trying to lead you and straighten your path, giving you joy. Look to him for the way.

PRAYERFULLY THINK ABOUT YOUR OWN LIFE WITH GOD:

I would venture to say that as you look back in your life, there have been times when God had to be patient with you. Perhaps you have strayed away from His truth now? When did you choose to do what you wanted to do other than what you knew the Lord wanted for you? Have you found another focus in your life which has become more important than God? If this happened in the past, do you regret those times now? Did they hurt you along the way? Are you thankful for the patience of God? Look back. Pray for God to show you your life as it truly is. Then write what you are thinking about now.

A Song of
God's Grace

Oh Soul are you weary and troubled?
No light in the darkness you see?
- Helen H. Lemmel

*V*ery depressed and trying to make sense of my life, God, and the universe, I asked my roommate, Barb, if she would go with me back to Augustana to talk with the chaplain. I had known him while we were in college. I don't know why I thought that would help, but Barb agreed to go. When we arrived in Rock Island, the chaplain couldn't see me. Wasn't that a "kick me when I'm down" moment? What do girls do when plans fall apart? Of course! We went downtown for a bit of shopping therapy.

There were Jesus people on all the corners passing out pamphlets and talking with passersby. They were part of the hippie generation of the 1960s and 70s, but they had put their faith in God instead of drugs. They often dressed in jeans and colorful tops, girls sometimes sporting flowers in their hair. Their belief in Jesus was strong enough for them to travel from place to place together to share their faith with those passing by on the streets. Barb and I spotted a cute guy on the opposite corner. We were on our way to talk to him when perhaps the ugliest man I have ever met stopped us. Barry's hair was long and dirty, he was missing teeth, and he talked in a scratchy drawl which made me cringe. "Do you girls know Jesus?" he asked.

"I've gone to church all of my life," I said as if I had all the answers.

"Oh, I'm so happy that you know the Lord. Jesus means everything to me after I accepted Him into my heart. I was really a lost sinner. I did nothing to deserve God's grace, but Jesus saved me anyway. God bless you both," he said as we quickly escaped.

Barb and I went to a coffee shop for some lunch. My mind was racing and kept going back to this ugly little man. He had nothing going for him. His clothes and hair were filthy. For goodness sakes, he had no teeth! And yet, in his eyes... there it was. I could see real joy - a peace and joy that I had been searching for since my freshman year in college. Could it be that Jesus could be real in my everyday life? Could it be that through grace, God did give sinful mankind a bridge to salvation through Jesus? I was remembering what I had learned over the years in church and Sunday school. Was God reaching out His hand to me today through this little man named Barry? Were some of my questions being answered?

I thought, *"God, if Jesus can give joy like that to Barry and just perhaps to a sinner like me, then that is what I need! It is more than going to church. It is Jesus!"* At that moment, it was like Jesus pulled up a chair to the table and put His arms around me. Never before had I experienced this sensation. I felt the Holy Spirit enter me and give me that same peace and joy that I had seen in Barry's eyes. All else in the world was dim. My questions melted away, and I <u>knew</u> God. A sense of awe filled my soul!!

Amid my joy, I heard Barb say, "Did you just feel what I felt?" Can you even imagine how my heart leaped when I heard that question from across the table? At that very moment, we had both experienced a divine touch of the Lord. Miraculously, we had found the Lord deep in our hearts at the same time! Excitement! Joy!! Looking at each other, we jumped up from the table and went running out to find Barry. He wasn't on the corner anymore.

As I look back on that experience, it is one of God's many mysteries to me. I had known God. Yet, that day brought the clear knowledge that God is there giving joy amid Earth's chaos. Barb has often asked me over the years why our encounter with God in Rock Island happened. We didn't do anything in particular to deserve it or make it happen. It was God's gift of true faith in Him that was simply given to us that day on April 15, 1972. God's grace alone. His grace rescues us from spiritual blindness. Today, I often think of the words of my favorite hymn written by a blind Helen Lemmel, words that were brought to life that day.

> *Turn your eyes upon Jesus. Look full in His wonderful face.*
> *And the things of Earth will grow strangely dim, in the light of His glory and grace.*[8]

Barry's face, Barry's eyes, had reflected the love of God through the Holy Spirit.

I am so thankful to God for His amazing GRACE!

~~~~~~~~~~~~~~~~~~~~~~~~~~~

LET'S TALK ABOUT GOD'S GRACE:

So, what is God's Grace? According to the Bible, in God's creation from the time man with his free will first sinned, God has been

---

[8] Lemmel, Helen H., Copyright © 1922, "Turn Your Eyes Upon Jesus", in the Public Domain.

working out a way to bring the people he loves back into his kingdom and glory with him. Our loving God sent His beloved son to be a sacrifice to atone for all of our sins. The Bible says much about grace, and we find a great summary:

> For it is by grace you have been saved, through faith –
> and this is not from yourselves, it is the gift of God.
> **Ephesians 2:8 (NIV)**

Grace is a free gift from God accepted by each of us through faith in Jesus his Son. I had believed that Jesus was real and with me when I was confirmed in 8th grade. It was a very immature acknowledgment. I knew facts and Bible verses, but I didn't know them in my heart. I didn't have sure knowledge that God was real. It was a religious acceptance, not a heart-changing sureness. After struggles in life, my realization that Jesus was <u>truly</u> there for me came in a café in Rock Island, Illinois. It is there that we began our true Father-daughter relationship.

Everyone has their own journey toward acceptance of the gift that God has sacrificed for us through the death and resurrection of His son, Jesus Christ. My mom freely accepted God's grace and salvation as a child, and the Holy Spirit guided her during her entire life. Others may be going to church, but it has become more of a social club until God leads them to understand that He is there for them in a much greater way. They have been missing something which others have found in Jesus. Maybe you have thought of church as a place of rules and regulations and woe to the person who breaks those rules. God's true church is free from the law. Jesus came to offer us grace just as we are. When our perception of ourselves changes and we feel lost and alone, we realize a place of humility. We cannot solve our own problems by ourselves. When we accept that Jesus is real and He did lay down his life for us, the

Holy Spirit will help us to grow closer to God and find the direction He wants us to take.

Jesus was a great teacher but much more. He was God's gift to the world – the Son of God. Hear his own words. When on trial before Pilate before his crucifixion, Jesus was asked:

> "So You are the Son of God?" And He said to them, "You say correctly that I am."
>
> **Luke 22:70 (NASB)**

Whether you are a regular churchgoer or go infrequently, you may have asked the same question of Jesus:"Who are you?" There is hope in the historic Jesus.

God wants to give us all the peace that passes understanding. Sometimes we go to church all of our lives, and we never really get to the "meat" of God's grace. We are still stuck on baby food and the stories we heard as a child. Once you step out in faith that Jesus was whom he said He was in history and ask forgiveness for sins, then God sends His Holy Spirit to dwell in you forever.. to be with you through the good and tough times to come. True Grace!! And it's free!!

KEY TO FINDING GOD'S JOY #3:

Make sure that you are not just going to church as a ritual. We are not perfect. Even for the most devoted Christians, there is always a chance to fall back into routine. We can lose sight of God, his grace, and his glory. Be aware and always thankful when you believe in and accept the grace of God through faith in his Son, Christ Jesus. You have a relationship with God. You are his son or daughter.

PRAYERFULLY THINK ABOUT YOUR OWN LIFE WITH GOD:

When did you find the true joy of knowing Jesus and the Holy Spirit through grace in your life? For many of you, it may have been long ago or as a child. Think about that time. Find the wonder of it! Wow! If you haven't found that joy, what can you do about accepting God's free gift of grace? Are you turned off by churchgoers who don't seem to really care? Are you turned off by the legalism and rules you believe some churches are promoting? Many of you may already realize that knowing Jesus is not about the law and rules. It is about having a relationship with Him. If you know Jesus this way through God's grace, do you depend on Him to get you through the good and bad of life? Or, do you find yourself falling back and relying on yourself rather than God's grace and strength to help you in your life? Think about those times. What can you do to change this? Do you talk to Him? When? Do you learn from his word, the Bible? Would others see the Holy Spirit and God's grace in your eyes and actions as we did in Barry's eyes? This is your time to ask yourself some of these questions. Take a few moments to write some of your thoughts about God's grace and relationship in your life.

_____

_____

_____

_____

_____

_____

_____

_____

A Song of
God's Spiritual Gifts

Breathe on me, Breath of God.
Fill me with life anew.
- Edwin Hatch and Robert Jackson

Barry! Barb's and my life had been completely renewed and changed, and we had hoped to find him on the corner in Rock Island. When we didn't find him, we heard that the Jesus people were having a tent meeting at a park in Rock Island down by the Mississippi River that night. Wanting to find and thank Barry, what do you think we did? We walked through that tent entrance into unknown territory. The group was charismatic and very different from what Barb or I had ever experienced. Hands were raised. People were praising God out loud. This Lutheran girl was out of her element, and so was my dear Presbyterian Barb. There were songs and a message, and then the pastor said, "God be with you now. Come forward if you feel the Lord leading you to accept Christ or a spiritual gift."

I was so overwhelmed with clarity, assurance, and gratitude to God for the gift of His Son and the experience of the day. Barb and I both walked to the front. The preacher prayed, some spoke in tongues in words you could not understand, and the meeting was over. There

24

was great joy in the tent. We left the meeting without ever seeing Barry again, now calling him Barry Angel.

Barb was driving as we started for home, and we excitedly talked about the blessing we had experienced. We praised God together for the miracle we had received.

"Everything I read in the Bible was true!" Barb said. "Thank you, Jesus!"

"Why didn't we realize God's power before this?" I asked.

I was quiet, thinking about God's overwhelming gift to me on that day. I had known God, but I hadn't known Him in this deep way in my soul. All of a sudden in the silence of the car, unrecognizable words began to flow from my soul through my voice. I was not trying to speak. The words flowed, and I was not in charge. I believe the Holy Spirit was praying through me and for me and probably for Barb in those moments. I had been given the gift of tongues. I did not know it at the time, but there are many spiritual gifts that the Lord bestows on his believers. Paul, in his First Letter to the Corinthians Chapter 12, describes the different spiritual gifts coming from God and the Holy Spirit. This was a breath from God within me. This was truly a gift from God as the hymn, *Breathe on Me, Breath of God* emphasizes.

> *Breathe on me breath of God. Fill me with life anew,*
> *that I may love what Thou dost love, and do what Thou*
> *wouldst do...*
> *Breathe on me, Breath of God, till I am wholly Thine,*
> *until this earthly part of me glows with Thy fire divine.*[9]

---

[9] Hatch, Edwin (words), Copyright © 1878, in the Public Domain, and Robert Jackson (music), Copyright © 1894, "Breathe on Me, Breath of God", in the Public Domain.

As I think back on it though, I have to giggle. In our churches, we had never been exposed to the spiritual gifts from God, and Barb became so stunned by the experience that she thought perhaps she should pull the car over to the side of the road. This was a holy moment, but we were not used to this gift. I would stop speaking for a few moments, Barb would breathe a big sigh of relief, and then the Holy Spirit had a few more words to say to God. In the midst of it, we would laugh with joy but also feel awe. Finally, I fell silent. God truly gave me a gift that night - much more than the gift of tongues. When I fell silent, I felt cleansed, free of all worry, guilt, or sadness, free from my sins, free from the pain of death, and totally resting in God's hands. A true blessing!

~~~~~~~~~~~~~~~~~~~~~~~~~~~~

LET'S TALK ABOUT GOD'S SPIRITUAL GIFTS:

I have never known of other friends who have come to personally know the Lord through the Holy Spirit at the <u>exact same moment</u> in such a mighty heart-changing way. For the prior five years, I had been unhappy, questioning, doubting, and seeking to know truth and peace. The prior five years, Barb had been in the happiest days of her life. Perhaps that is why God chose to fill us with the Holy Spirit at the same moment. If I had been alone, I might have thought I was simply overcome with emotion, because I had been in such a bad place and had grabbed onto whatever was near to comfort me. Perhaps if Barb had been alone, her analytical mind would have dismissed it as something that couldn't have logically happened. And yet it did, and the miracle changed us both forever. I came to this place through facing true death, doubt, and possible self-destruction. With all I had done, I did not deserve God's salvation or the blessing of the Holy Spirit praying for me. And yet, God used those tough times in my life to bring me to the foot of the cross, with forgiveness, peace, and true joy.

Do I live in that high emotional miraculous state most days? Many times, I do live very close to God, but sometimes, I find I can only cling to that still small voice in my soul that lets me know for sure that God is there. I have only spoken in tongues one other time in my life, and it is still God's mystery to me.

The Bible describes the many different gifts of the Holy Spirit:

> Now to each one the manifestation of the Spirit is given for the common good. To one there is given through the Spirit a message of wisdom, to another a message of knowledge by means of the same Spirit, to another faith by the same Spirit, to another gifts of healing by that one Spirit, to another miraculous powers, to another prophecy, to another distinguishing between spirits, to another speaking in different kinds of tongues, and to still another the interpretation of tongues. All these are the work of one and the same Spirit, and He distributes them to each one, just as He determines.
> **1st Corinthians 12:7–11 (NIV)**

In other places in the Bible, God mentions the spiritual gifts of teaching, leadership, and hospitality.

After Jesus died on the cross and rose again, leaving the tomb empty, he appeared to his disciples.

> On the evening of that first day of the week, when the disciples were together, with the doors locked for fear of the Jewish leaders, Jesus came and stood among them and said, "Peace be with you!" After He said this, He

showed them his hands and side. The disciples were overjoyed when they saw the Lord. Again Jesus said, "Peace be with you! As the Father has sent me, I am sending you." And with that He breathed on them and said, "Receive the Holy Spirit."

John 20:19–22 (NIV)

After Jesus had gone to Heaven, the day of Pentecost came and the crowds were confused by the disciples speaking in different languages:

Peter replied, "Repent and be baptized, every one of you, in the name of Jesus Christ for the forgiveness of your sins. And you will receive the gift of the Holy Spirit."

Acts 2:38 (NIV)

When we do not even know what to pray and how to help ourselves in different situations, we can ask the Holy Spirit to pray for us or to give us the words to express what we are feeling to God:

In the same way, the Spirit helps us in our weakness. We do not know what we ought to pray for, but the Spirit Himself intercedes for us with wordless groans.

Romans 8:26 (NIV)

KEY TO FINDING THE JOY OF GOD #4:

God has sent the Holy Spirit to all who believe in the Lord Jesus. Each one has received different gifts from the Holy Spirit. It may be the gift of tongues. It may be another gift. If you go to church but don't feel led by the Holy Spirit, perhaps you haven't noticed that God's Spirit is within you. Then tap into the Spirit and ask the Lord to fill you with the Holy Spirit. For those who already know the Holy

Spirit, stretch yourself to be aware of his nudges. Not only does the Spirit give gifts to those who know Him, but it is the Spirit who will transform you, teach you, and guide you as you grow. It is the Spirit who will help you find joy deep in your soul even in weak tough times.

PRAYERFULLY THINK ABOUT YOUR OWN LIFE WITH GOD:

When did you receive Jesus as your Savior? If you were very young, you may not have even understood how the Spirit comes to dwell in the hearts of those He has saved though grace. If you knew nothing of the Bible, perhaps you didn't realize that you have received power in the Holy Spirit which resides in your soul. Do you sometimes feel the Lord leading you in a certain direction or nudging you to do something? That is the Holy Spirit within you. Listen and learn from the Holy Spirit. What has been your experience with the Holy Spirit? You do not have to be charismatic to experience the leading of the Spirit. For many of you, God's Spirit has been leading you for a long time. You know the gifts he has given you. Perhaps to find God's joy again, take a step today to remember how the Holy Spirit is gifting you and transforming you. Stretch yourself to use the gifts the Spirit has given you to help others each day. Helping always brings joy. If you have not experienced the Holy Spirit in your life, what can you do about this? You can ask the Holy Spirit to come in a mighty way. "Spirit of the living God, please allow me to learn from you. Fall afresh on me." When you are in a bad place, have you ever asked the Spirit to pray for you? It may not be a gift of tongues, but we know the Holy Spirit will pray for us in our time of need. Ask Him. Take a few moments and reflect on the Holy Spirit and your relationship with this member of the Triune God.

A Song of
God's Guidance

Be Thou my wisdom, be Thou my true word.
- Eleanor H. Hull and Mary E. Byrne

The joy! You can't even imagine the pure joy! God had transformed Barb and me, and we couldn't stop talking about Jesus. We read the Bible constantly.

"Hey, Barb. Will you read the Bible out loud while I iron?"

"Let me read the Bible while you wash the dishes, Barb." We couldn't get enough of God's word for us. When it gets down to building your faith in God, His word in the Bible is the way God will speak to you.

Barb even called her sister, Linda, who was in seminary to ask why she hadn't told Barb how wonderful it was to truly know the Lord. We just couldn't get our fill of learning about Jesus. More! We needed to know more. I don't think we really had a sense that it would take a lifetime of learning about Jesus and that he would always be teaching us.

We went to a Bible Study which Barb's parents attended to let them know what had happened to us. It was as if we thought we were the only Christians in the world. Saying we were kind of obnoxious is an understatement! We were new in Christ. We didn't know how to share or empathize or take our first steps toward helping others know the joy in Christ. We enthusiastically told friends what had happened. A few were scared away. Actor Denzel Washington described the excitement he had after he became a Christian and truly was filled with the Holy Spirit. He said he was so excited that he performed "spiritual muggings" on his friends. Newly excited Christians are sometimes guilty of that, but only out of love for their friends or relatives. I was guilty of that.

Visiting the pastors of Barb's parents' church, we talked to them about what had happened to us. Their response? "You two really need some training."

Pastor Cal and Pastor Paul told of a group called Youth with a Mission (YWAM). "This group sends youth around the world to different locations to share the gospel message with others. There is a group training at a mission in Chicago this summer. Perhaps you would like to join them?"

That summer vacation from school, we joined YWAM. The training in the Chicago mission gave us some insight into sharing our faith. We went out on the streets of Chicago to share the gospel with strangers. After completing our training, we flew to Munich, Germany. Further training took place in a beautiful castle in Hurlach. Our YWAM group learned from ministers of the gospel. We also read books by authors such as Francis Schaeffer's *The God Who Is There*[10] and also C.S. Lewis' *Mere Christianity*[11]. These books helped us to develop what the Lord had started in Rock Island. When we first experienced the Holy Spirit in that café, it was sure

---

[10] Schaeffer, Francis A., Copyright © 1968, *The God Who Is There,* by L'Abri Fellowship, InterVarsity Press, Downers Grove, IL (2020).
[11] Lewis, C.S., Copyright © 1952, *Mere Christianity*, Geoffrey Bles (UK), New York, NY, Macmillan Publishers (US).

personal knowledge of Jesus' reality and presence that we felt. At Hurlach, we built on what we had already learned from Sunday School and church.

In Francis A. Schaeffer's book, *The God Who Is There,* he challenges all of us to think of the Jesus of history: "What does it mean to believe on, to cast oneself on, Christ? I would suggest there are four crucial aspects to be considered... The individual must come to a positive conclusion and affirmation concerning them, if he is to believe in the Biblical sense:

1. Do you believe that God exists and that He is a personal God, and that Jesus Christ is God – remembering that we are not talking about the *word* or *idea* god, but of the infinite personal God who is there?

2. Do you acknowledge that you are guilty in the presence of God - remembering that we are not talking about guilt feelings but true moral guilt?

3. Do you believe that Jesus Christ died in space and time in history on the cross, and that when he died His substitutional work of bearing God's punishment against sin was fully accomplished and complete?

4. On the basis of God's promises in his communication to us, the Bible, do you (or have you) cast yourself on this Christ as your personal Savior – not trusting in anything you yourself have ever done or ever will do?

My faith is simply the empty hands by which I accept God's free gift."[12]

---

[12] Republished with permission of InterVarsity Press, Downers Grove, IL (2020), from *The God Who Is There,* Francis A. Schaeffer, Copyright © 1968 by L'Abri Fellowship, p. 134-135; permission conveyed through Copyright Clearance Center, Inc.

These words now made perfect sense to us. After our classes, we were ready to spread across Germany to different army posts.

We prayed about our assignment. I had many questions at this time. "What if God wants me to go someplace that I don't want to go?" I remember asking that question to one of our teachers.

"If God wants you to go there, he will give you peace in your heart about that calling." I was not just talking about this time in Germany. I was thinking of becoming a missionary, and the thought of God asking me to go to a very dangerous place was scary. For then, I simply had to pray about where in Germany the Lord wanted me to minister. I prayed and kept coming up with the letter "A". That was all I could get. Groups of six formed. We were to go to Army posts in Germany to build coffee houses. There we would share and minister to young men and women on the posts. My assignment was in Aschaffenburg, Germany.

On the army post in Aschaffenburg, I am standing under our sign outside of our coffee house which we called "The Door".

It was kind of comical as to where Barb and I ministered. Just before we accepted the Lord, I had been miserable in my life, and it was as if God said, *"Susan, you need a break."* My assignment in Aschaffenburg placed me in a lovely apartment with the chaplain on base and his family. I had my own room with a nice bathroom. It was all very comfortable.

Barb, who had life pretty good before our trip to Rock Island, was in Butzbach in a very old building that was once a sewing factory. Her team lived in the attic and had no facilities for bathing or washing clothes. They had a long walk to the army base on dusty roads to take baths and wash clothes in someone's home once a week. I experienced this when I visited Barb in Butzbach. We hiked to the assigned home, and I couldn't wait for my turn to bathe. I winced as I saw the tub. The same bath water was shared by several people until it was time for the washing machine water to empty into the tub. Then, the last person had to be out. The team walked back to the factory with their wet clothes which they hung to almost never dry on a line strung across the attic ceiling. A miserable experience!!

Barb and I were two examples of joy amid ease and the other amid hardship. However, we were both able to share the gospel message that God loved each one who was coming to our coffee houses. Those men and women who came needed to feel our love. God guided us to this realization as we ministered on the army bases. God showed us His vision for how we were to change our ways and become His vessels of love. We welcomed everyone to our coffee houses. With every person who came, we talked about their lives and what was important to them. We tried to help them feel loved and safe in our surroundings. We had built the coffee house, because we wanted to share love with each and every one. We did fun activities such as hikes which brought the group together in joy. Conversations did come up about the Lord after a relationship had been established. We cared about what each person was experiencing in life. It was all about God and not about us. How can I not think of the hymn, *Be Thou My Vision?*

> *Be Thou my vision O Lord of my heart. Naught be all*
> *else to me save that Thou art.*
> *Thou my best thought by day or by night; waking or*
> *sleeping,*
> *Thy presence my light.*
> *Be Thou my wisdom; be Thou my true Word. I ever with*
> *Thee,*
> *and Thou with me Lord.*
> *Thou my great Father. I Thy true son. Thou in me*
> *dwelling,*
> *and I with Thee one.* [13]

~~~~~~~~~~~~~~~~~~~~~~~~~~~~~~

LET'S TALK ABOUT GOD'S GUIDANCE:

After you initially come to know Jesus as Savior and Lord, the Holy Spirit guides you and transforms you in His ways. The experience in Germany taught us a bit more about how to share our testimonies.

> Jesus replied: "Love the Lord your God with all your
> heart and with all your soul and with all your mind. This
> is the first and greatest commandment. And the second
> is like it: Love your neighbor as yourself."
>
> **Matthew 22:37-39 (NIV)**

---

[13] Hull, Eleanor H. (versifier), Mary E. Byrne (translator of old Irish hymn, "Bi Thusa 'mo Shúle", ca 700 A.D.), Copyright © 1905, "Be Thou My Vision", in the Public Domain.

Sharing God's love was the key, not just sharing our personal experiences in finding Him. How can we share God's love in our circle of friends, neighbors, and strangers? God wants us to be kind to all, be helpful to those in need, empathize with others' problems, and try hard to put ourselves in their shoes. We especially need to be good listeners not only to them but to what God is saying to us about them. Stepping out of our churches and treating all we meet with love and respect is also key. Be hospitable. Think of how you would feel love from someone's actions. If you have pain in your life, put it in God's hands and find His joy and peace. However, be real. This does not mean putting on a false front. It is not false if God has given you His peace and joy amid your pain. Others will notice you have reacted differently than most.

We are wholly saved through the death and intercession of Jesus on our behalf. We are part of His kingdom, and there is great joy in seeing what God has in store for us on our journey. As Jesus said:

> As the Father has loved me, so have I loved you. Now remain in my love. If you keep my commands, you will remain in my love, just as I have kept My Father's commands and remain in His love. I have told you this so that My joy may be in you and that your joy may be complete. My command is this: Love each other as I have loved you.
>
> **John 15:9-12 (NIV)**

Joy is complete when we love the Lord who loves all. If we are obedient, we love others and that means all others. We do not need to like what some others do, but we need to still love them and show them our love through the power of the Holy Spirit. Pray to the Lord to ask Him how to love another. *"What is it, Lord, that this person needs from You and from me? How can I best show them Your love?*

Do they need a listening ear? Do they need food or clothing? Let them see Your love light shining through my eyes."

KEY TO FINDING GOD'S JOY #5:

As a Christian, always seek the guidance of the Lord through prayer in all you do. The best ideas you may have might not be God's best in the situation. Let Him be your compass in all that you do. Love all those you encounter. You can share your testimony, but only when God inspires you to do so at His right timing. Listen to the prompting and guidance of the Holy Spirit. Joy will come in your close dependence on God and in the help you can give another. Giving almost always brings more joy than receiving.

PRAYERFULLY THINK ABOUT YOUR OWN LIFE WITH GOD:

Have you ever had an experience when someone else came on too strongly to you? Perhaps it was before you were a Christian. Maybe it wasn't even about Christianity, but it was about another topic. Did it help or did it turn you off? Have you ever been the overwhelming one in sharing your story of your coming to the Lord with others? How did that work out for you? As you see in my journey, God needs to be our guide in what we say and how we say it. In reality, God wants us to simply show love to those around us, whether Christians or not. It is the Holy Spirit that will work through that love to touch the hearts of those to whom we speak. How do you share the love of the Lord? Have you had the experience of the "nudge" from the Lord in showing love to someone? What happened? You can freely share the testimony of your experience with God. Just make sure you are led by the Holy Spirit to share. Once again, take a few moments to reflect on your experience in ignoring or finding God's guidance in sharing His love with someone else.

A Song of Joy in God

God is so good!
- Anonymous

*M*ission field! Here we come! When Barb and I returned from YWAM to Illinois, we felt led to move from our apartment in Wheaton, IL to International Village, a place having the reputation of being a swinging singles complex in Lombard. The CBS television show "60 Minutes" had even done a segment on the wild Village singles. We hoped to show God's love to our neighbors. Perhaps they would be able to see the love of Jesus in our eyes.

There were many buildings, and on the day we were to move in, I ran in to get the keys. There was a glitch. The apartment we were to take wasn't available, but there was an apartment clear across the campus which we could have. Do you think God can use or perhaps even orchestrate the glitches in our lives?

Barb and I pulled up to the new building. Outside in the parking lot was a man, fairly short and stocky with tousled hair. He was wearing jean shorts and bright neon blue sunglasses, holding a six-pack of beer as he smoked his cigarette.

"Are you girls moving in?" he asked. When we replied in the affirmative, he and his roommate helped us move to the apartment right above his. We shared that place with another friend, Joan. Andy was very outgoing, cracking jokes and telling stories. His giant laugh was infectious.

"Do you want to come to a party at my place tonight?" Yes we sure did. And so that night we went to his apartment for the party. We had just met the man who threw most of the parties in the entire complex.

I don't remember the first conversation about the Lord that we had with Andy. I do remember that Andy sensed we were different from his normal party-going group. We became good friends with him. We loved Andy.

Barb speculated, "If Andy came to know the Lord in his heart, everyone in this apartment complex would know about it."

Andy would knock on our door and immediately say, "We aren't going to talk about the Lord tonight." He would then continue to ask us questions about Jesus. He was seeking, just as I had sought answers to many questions about God in prior years. (Of course, I am always asking God questions to this day!)

One night, we heard a knock on the door. Andy practically ran into our apartment! The Lord had turned his life upside down. "I prayed that Jesus would come into my heart, and I can't believe how great this is!" Andy was miraculously changed. He was filled with joy! God had done a mighty work, and now Andy was the obnoxious one!

We were right. Everyone in the complex started to hear about the change in Andy's life. Instead of inviting friends to parties at his apartment, it was, "Hey! Do you want to come to a Bible study by the pond in the complex tonight?" At these meetings by the pond, we would share, pray, and sing. Barb would play the guitar. One of our favorite easy-to-sing songs for brand new Christians was *God Is So Good*. The lyrics were very simple.

> *God is so good. God is so good. God is so good. He's so good to me.*
> Other verses included, *He cares for me. He answers prayers,* and more.[14]

We left flyers about the Bible study at many doors throughout the complex. Young singles came - some out of curiosity, some seeking. Many became Christians.

Knowing we all needed teaching, we started to caravan from Lombard to Aurora at 1st Presbyterian Church. This was Barb's parents' church. When walking in for the first time, many of us were amazed by the beautiful stained-glass windows and the big organ pipes up in front. After all, we had been meeting in apartments or by the pond at International Village. We all went right up to the front where the good seats were still available.

Pastor Cal watched us come in. "This is the nightclub crowd who always wants the front seats at a concert," he said.

Barb's parents established a singles ministry at the Hilton Inn in Aurora, and our group from Lombard merged with other young people from Aurora to learn more about the Lord. Joining our group were Andy's 4 old friends from high school in Lombard who came to know Jesus as a result of seeing the change in Andy. One of these men, Dan, eventually married Barb. Andy and the other three, Kit,

---

[14]Anonymous, "God Is So Good", in the Public Domain.

Jack, and Skip, all went on to seminary and became ministers of the gospel. "Unshackled", a radio show recorded by the Pacific Garden Mission and on the Chicago WMBI radio station, did a four-part series of dramas - one for the change God had brought into each of the four men's lives.

Our Bible study group at International Village began to think about the larger community in the western suburbs of Chicago. "The Exorcist" movie was released in theaters. We worried that people would be scared, alone, and questioning the existence of God. Our group spent many nights passing out flyers to those in line waiting to see the movie at the Oak Brook theater. These flyers included Bible scripture:

> Peace I leave with you; My peace I give you. I do not give to you as the world gives. Do not let your hearts be troubled and do not be afraid.
>
> **John 14:27 (NIV)**

We also gave them information to call a phone number at our apartment, if they were scared after the movie or if they had questions. I sometimes answered the phone in the middle of the night and had a good conversation. They usually asked how I knew that Jesus was really God. Unfortunately, after talking with the person who was calling, I often went back to bed and forgot what had been said. It was not one of my proudest moments in God's service. I do remember that most people calling were very timid, and I sensed they were afraid. Some asked why we were passing out the flyers. Some wanted to ask about God, and we had a conversation about the love of God for them. I pray each of those people who called turned to God for peace.

This was a great time of joy in my life! The Holy Spirit truly worked through love in the lives of our neighbors at International Village. Can God use a glitch in your life or what?!!!

~~~~~~~~~~~~~~~~~~~~~~~~~~~~~~~~~

LET'S TALK ABOUT JOY IN GOD:

When we come to know the Lord, we do not become perfect. God has forgiven our sins and has sent the Holy Spirit to teach us and to help us grow. All will NOT go smoothly. If I had not experienced the suffering during the deaths of two boyfriends, would I have found the joy described in what happened in this chapter? Probably not. That is not to say that God caused those two deaths to bring me to this point. Bad things happen in this world to all of us. It is the way of a fallen world. However, God can bring joy to us even in the worst of circumstances. It is the knowledge that He is with us and the peace He gives us deep in our hearts.

> You make known to me the path of life; You will fill me with joy in Your presence, with eternal pleasures at Your right hand.
>
> **Psalm 16:11 (NIV)**

There is joy in seeing friends and relatives and strangers also come to know who Jesus is and accept His invitation to new life in Him. There is a wonderful joy in seeing the miracle of that multiplication in the numbers of those who are living a life of love, joy, and peace in the Lord.

Do you know that God works in mysterious ways? The church which my husband and I attend now, Westminster Presbyterian Church in Aurora, IL, is in the process of finding a new pastor. Our transition pastor, Jeff, is one of the finest men of God I have ever known. Every week, his word for us from God left us thinking and thanking God for who He truly is in our lives. Jeff recently was offered a new job that, through God's grace, seems to be a perfect fit for him. However, all of us at church were heartbroken to see him move on in God's plan for him.

You will never guess who is filling our need for a pastor until God brings His new plan for us. God brought us Andy! Yes! Andy, whom Barb and I met at International Village almost 50 years ago, is now a retired minister. He has found his way to our church in this time of our need. When he gave his first sermon, I cried through the entire message. I had never heard Andy preach. His message was one of encouragement and of how God works in ways we cannot even imagine. Throughout five or six accounts of the Bible, Andy told of the multiple-choice answers which man would have thought to be true and in the end, what God thought to be true.

Andy told of Moses and the Israelites being chased by the Egyptian pharaoh's men. Then, they had a real problem. They came to the Red Sea and were trapped. Choices (I paraphrase):

A. They could stand and fight.

B. They could surrender and say they had just lost their minds for a bit. They would happily go back now and continue as slaves in Egypt.

C. They could swim for it, but this would mean leaving all their goods behind.

D. None of the above.

God had a plan for them. D. None of the above. Instead, He parted the Red Sea, and they were able to walk across with all of their animals and goods.

Another example from Andy was just how the Messiah was to enter Jerusalem as God's answer for man's separation from God - as the Son of God. (Once again a paraphrase):

A. Jesus would come with an army of men to conquer Jerusalem and the Romans.

B. Jesus would use His power of God to strike down the enemy and take the city.

C. Jesus would show miracles and God's power and every knee would bow.

D. None of the above.

God's plan was D. None of the above. Instead, Jesus chose to ride into Jerusalem on a lowly donkey. He did not fight. He knew he was fulfilling the Father's plan for him. Jesus was to die on the cross for our sins. He was to bring all to saving grace, being restored into glory with God if they would accept it. He had humbled himself and come to be a sacrifice for all of our sins.

Many years ago, God used a glitch in Barb and my lives to bring Andy to accept Jesus as his Lord and Savior. On this day, God brought hope and joy to me by using Andy to bring God's word to us. A full-circle moment! What an amazing God we have! I am filled with joy!

One thing that joy is NOT: Spiritual joy in God is not all happiness. In the most unhappy times in my life, I have felt the joy of the Lord getting me through each day. It has been awe and confidence that God is with me no matter what I have done or what the situation may be that I am experiencing at the time.

I came upon a blog quote which I loved:

"True joy is a limitless, life-defining, transformative reservoir waiting to be tapped into. It requires the utmost surrender and, like love, is a choice to be made. Joy is not simply a feeling that happens...

- Joy is in the heart. Happiness is on the face.

- Joy is of the soul. Happiness is of the moment.

- Joy transcends. Happiness reacts."[15]

Author C.S. Lewis lived his entire young life into adulthood struggling to find joy. He was an atheist. His journey to come to know God as Lord began with a fireside chat. Lewis wrote, "Early in 1926 the hardest boiled of all the atheists I ever knew sat in my room on the other side of the fire and remarked that the evidence for the historicity of the Gospels was really surprisingly good. 'Rum thing', he went on. 'All that stuff of Frazer's about the Dying God. Rum thing. It almost looks as if it had really happened once.'"[16] This started C.S. Lewis thinking about what he had once called "Christian Mythology". Was it really a myth? Lewis also realized, "There was no doubt that Joy was a desire... But a desire is turned not to itself but to its object. Not only that, but it owes all its character to its object."[17] C.S. Lewis had concluded that it is the object that brings us joy. It is looking to the Lord as our object of joy in good or bad times.

---

[15] https://www.compassion.com/sponsor_a_child/difference-between-joy-and-happiness.htm, viewed on June 17, 2022.
[16] *Surprised by Joy – The Shape of My Early Years* by C.S. Lewis © Copyright CS Lewis Pte Ltd 1955, Page 273. Extract used with permission.
[17] *Surprised by Joy – The Shape of My Early Years* by C.S. Lewis © Copyright CS Lewis Pte Ltd 1955, Pages 268-269. Extract used with permission.

When we can look at our lives that way, what comes to us that brings us joy?

1. The love of God through the Holy Spirit! He is with us!

2. Excitement that others just have to share the great love of Jesus.

3. Joy amid big problems now attacked in new ways with help from the Holy Spirit.

4. Hearts at peace a day at a time.

5. Love for others!

There is nothing better in this world than the joy of the Lord!

KEY TO FINDING GOD'S JOY #6:

Find your joy in the Lord in good times but even when you go through hard times. Dig into that transformative reservoir. The Spirit is there with you, giving you peace and love one day at a time. Cling to that through faith and spread the good news to others when led by the Holy Spirit to share. God wants others to find his joy!

PRAYERFULLY THINK ABOUT YOUR OWN LIFE WITH GOD:

There is no doubt that we can find joy in the good times. It is quite different to think of finding joy and peace in difficult times. God is not standing afar from us and striking us with those hard times. The good and the bad happen to all of us in this fallen world. But God can take those difficult times and find gifts of joy in the middle of them all. Have you accepted that your suffering in life is part of God's good plan for you if you look to Him in the midst of it? If not, what might you try? Perhaps you could listen for that still small voice that says, "*I am here throughout this tough time. Rest in Me. I will give you peace.*"

Listen to that voice and allow the Holy Spirit to bring you that peace and joy through prayer. If you go to church but have not found joy in the Lord, what might bring you into closer fellowship with Jesus and the Holy Spirit? Do you pray to God and share your problems? Just talking to Him will help. Do you read the Bible for guidance? I pray you are experiencing the joy of the Lord in the happiest times of your life, as well. Sometimes it is easy to ignore God when all is happy and easy. Have you experienced the nudge of the Lord to share His love with others? Are there ways that you can care about and give hope to others? Are others noticing that you are different in a way that makes them wonder? What joy you will find when others experience the joy of the Lord! What are your thoughts as you have read this chapter? Have you found the joy of the Lord? When have you found his joy and peace during a hard or a great time?

_____

_____

_____

_____

_____

_____

_____

_____

_____

_____

_____

7

A Song of
God's Provision

All you may need He will provide
God will take care of you
- Civilla Durfee Martin and Walter Stillman Martin

Strange things afoot! Tornado in the sky!! As I drove, it was a clear beautiful August day but there ahead of me was what looked like a white tornado in the sky. It seemed like such an unusual thing to see, and I couldn't imagine what it was. It did not look like a cloud formation but an actual swirling cone of white.

I had left Lombard, Illinois and was heading to my parents' home in Flushing, Michigan to visit in August. I had about an hour to go before arrival. The road I was on was a four-lane highway with all kinds of access roads and a large median in the middle of the two directions of the road. Cruising along in my yellow Volkswagen Beetle at the speed limit of 70 mph., I came up over a hill which also veered to the right, again saw the "tornado" before me in the sky, and BANG!!!! CRASH!!!!

Rolling over and bouncing off the road into the ditch, my car came to an upright stop. Oh, the pain! My abdomen hurt. Blood oozed from my face after my head hit the steering wheel. Pain in my mouth! My little Volkswagen with no engine in the front crushed in toward my legs.

I had worn my shoulder strap for the 4 ½ hours it had taken to get to the east side of Lansing, MI. Rubbing on my shoulder and very uncomfortable, I slipped the shoulder strap off my shoulder and left the seat belt in place. That seat belt saved my life. The missing shoulder strap allowed my head to hit the steering wheel.

A lady in a station wagon filled with children had stopped in the passing lane to turn left to get to a gas station. She had not pulled into the available median to wait for the crossing traffic to pass. I hit a stopped car while going 70 mph! I never saw the car before impact.

The doctor told me later if I had seen the car ahead of me, I would have braced for the impact and all of my leg bones could have shattered. I have always wondered if the strange white "tornado" I saw in the sky was a sign from God to protect me from broken leg bones through this trauma in my life.

Sitting in my car in the ditch, bleeding and in pain, I began to pray. I truly thought it was my time to meet the Lord in person. Crying and screaming sounds from children in the other car were all I could hear.

> *"Lord. Let the people in the other car be O.K. Be with Mom and Dad and my dear brother Jim and all my friends and family, Lord. Help them to depend on You when they find out about this. Be with Danny and help him to stop the drugs and find you. Be with him in prison now, Lord, and help him to find You in the Bible I gave him. I pray for all those who do not know You in their hearts yet. Thank you, God, for all You have done for me in bringing me Your saving grace. Thank you for my blessings! Be with me now in a mighty way."*

I was probably in shock, but I felt a great peace come over me. I looked out the window and a man was there. He gently took gauze and placed it over my chin and mouth. Who was this man who just happened to have gauze with him? An ambulance hadn't arrived yet. Perhaps two minutes later, I looked out my shattered window, and there was my mother!!

I knew immediately that this was God's provision for me to get through this terrible situation. Mom's job was to head a large senior travel program for the park district in Flint, Michigan. Once a week she took busloads of seniors to enjoy locations around the state. She was always on the lead bus. This day through God's providence, she was not. They had been visiting the Kellogg facilities in Battle Creek, Michigan and were running late. The lead bus driver had seen the accident in his rearview mirror and said if that car didn't stop, she would be a dead person. After my car had bounced into the ditch, Mom's bus came behind the lead bus. She recognized my yellow Volkswagen. She knew it was probably me because of the sticker I had in my back window which said, "I Am Eternally Grateful to Jesus".

Mom yelled to the bus driver, "Stop! That's my daughter!" She turned to her people on the bus. "Please pray for my daughter and me." She jumped off the bus, ran across the road, and was the first person I saw after my bloodied face had been covered. That was God's gift to my mom. That she was there at that moment was truly God's gift to me.

We rode to the hospital together in the ambulance.

Meanwhile, at home, my dad was about to go out and mow the lawn to make the home look good before his girl arrived. However, Dad did not go out to mow. He described it as a feeling which came to him that if something happened to me on my drive home, he would not get the call if he was outside. So he stayed inside, where he heard the call when it came. After getting the call from Mom, he was off to the hospital in Lansing.

Doctors had just inserted the feeding tube down into my stomach. I kept gagging and throwing up.

"Stop that throwing up!" yelled the doctor. "I can't stitch up your chin if you don't get that under control!"

It was all I could do to keep my stomach reflexes in check. Somehow, the chin was closed.

I had a gash on my chin, a broken jawbone, lost teeth, and injuries produced to my abdomen by the seatbelt. I had to spend time in the Intensive Care Unit before then being moved to a regular room. One really great blessing: every single person in the other car survived the accident.

"Heh heh heh! What are you doing here? You just had to wreck that new VW I just helped pick out with you!" said Andy as he and Barb and Dan walked into my hospital room. They had rented an airplane to fly them to Lansing, so they could be there before friends, Linda and Joan, made the drive. God's provision of loving friends! All now at International Village, the Hilton Singles Ministry, and 1st Presbyterian Church in Aurora were praying for my healing along with the prayers of my parents, members of their church, and all the seniors who knew Mom.

After a month of recuperating in Michigan, my friend Kit came to drive me back to Illinois. "Kit, let me share my favorite psalm with you," my mom said. My mom shared Psalm 139 which was a great comfort to her and to me at the time and a comfort to Andy's high school friend, a new Christian, Kit.

You have searched me, Lord, and You know me. You know when I sit and when I rise; You perceive my thoughts from afar. You discern my going out and my lying down; You are familiar with all my ways.

Psalm 139:1-3 (NIV)

God knew what we were going through in this time, and He was there with us.

I returned to Illinois for more recovery, and I was able to return to teaching in mid-October. Not fully recovered, it was a tough year of school, but God took care of me throughout this entire experience. The song that comes to mind is *God Will Take Care of You.*

> *All you may need He will provide, God will take care of you...*
> *Beneath His wings of love abide, God will take care of you.*[18]

Beneath the wings of God's love, I found my place of security and sanctuary that God gives us in troubled times. God's provisions of that crazy white "tornado", my mom's immediate appearance at the accident scene, my dad's word from the Holy Spirit about needing to stay indoors that day, and the friends and family to care and pray for me were all God's gifts to me during that difficult season. It was God alone! As my destroyed sticker in the window of my yellow VW Beetle said, "I Am Eternally Grateful to Jesus!"

~~~~~~~~~~~~~~~~~~~~~~~~~~~~~~~~

---

[18]Martin, Civilla Durfee (Words) and Walter Stillman Martin (Music), Copyright © 1904, "God Will Take Care of You", Words and Music in the Public Domain.

LET'S TALK ABOUT GOD'S PROVISIONS FOR US:

Has God provided for you in your life? God's provisions come in many forms. Have you believed that God only helps those who help themselves? We can pray and God can give us a way to help ourselves. Sometimes answered prayers come in the form of other people to help us. Provisions can come when we least expect them before we need them. And sometimes they come in the form of miracles. I believe my mom's appearance at my window right after my accident was God's miracle for me.

Sometimes God's provisions don't come in a way that we can see until time has passed, and we look back. "Oh! That's why that happened!"

We live in a fallen world where bad things happen to God's people as well as those who don't know Him. It is said that rain falls on everyone. When we experience trouble, it can be confusing to read in the Word:

> And we know that in all things God works for the good
> of those who love Him, who have been called according
> to His purpose.
>
> **Romans 8:28 (NIV)**

No one escapes the tough times in this world. Life as a Christian can be such a rollercoaster. At one moment you are on top of the world. At another moment, you are going through the everyday experiences with God at your side and in your heart. However, there are also times when you are clinging to that faint voice of God in your heart that tells you God is there even in the midst of the very difficult times of life. I believe that God does work all things for the good for those who love Him, because He loves us. He provides His Holy Spirit to be with us in our times of need. We may struggle to see the good. We may never see the good. But ultimately all the happiness of life and all the pains of life are incomparable to the love, hope, security, and power we have through the gift of God's grace in Jesus Christ and the Holy Spirit. Romans 8 continues:

> No, in all these things we are more than conquerors through Him who loved us. For I am convinced that neither death nor life, neither angels nor demons, neither the present nor the future, nor any powers, neither height nor depth, nor anything else in all creation, will be able to separate us from the love of God that is in Christ Jesus our Lord.
>
> **Romans 8:37-39 (NIV)**

This is why we can have joy and peace in times of trouble. Nothing, no nothing can separate us from God who loves us. He is always with us. His love is His greatest gift.

When I think of God bringing provisions and good out of tough times, I am always reminded of the life of Corrie Ten Boom. During the Nazi occupation of Corrie's hometown, Haarlem, Netherlands, she and her family as Christians helped to hide Jewish people in their home to help them escape. They were eventually found out by a Nazi spy who sent the Gestapo to their home to arrest them. Corrie and each person in the family had an escape bag. In it were warm clothes, toiletries, and a Bible. When the Nazis asked her to leave her room, she dared not pick up her escape bag. The hiding place of the Jews was behind a false wall in Corrie's bedroom, and her bag leaned against that wall. She left it so the officer's gaze would not go toward that false wall. The Jewish people in the hiding place were not found, but Corrie, her sister Betsie, her father, and other relatives were sent to prison where her father died within ten days. Betsie and Corrie eventually ended up in the Ravensbrúck women's labor concentration camp in Germany. Her story was made famous in the book, *The Hiding Place: The Triumphant True Story of Corrie Ten Boom*. It was Betsie who always seemed to be in prayerful thanksgiving for all that which God had blessed them. When entering their barracks at Ravensbrúck, Corrie was horrified that there were fleas in their beds and everywhere in the place.

Corrie wrote in her book:

"'Betsie how can we live in such a place!'

'Show us. Show us how.'

It was said so matter of factly that it took me a second to realize she was praying...

'Corrie!' she said excitedly. 'He's given us the answer! Before we asked, as He always does! In the Bible this morning. Where was it?...'

'It was in First Thessalonians,' I said... 'Here it is: Comfort the frightened, help the weak, be patient with everyone. See that none of you repay evil for evil, but always seek to do good to one another and to all.'

'Go on,' said Betsie. 'That wasn't all.'

'Oh yeah'... 'Rejoice always, pray constantly, give thanks in all circumstances, for this is the will in Christ Jesus...'

'Such as,' I said.

'Such as being assigned here together.'

I bit my lip. 'Oh yes, Lord Jesus.'

'Such as what you are holding in your hands.'

> I looked down at the Bible. 'Yes, thank you dear Lord that there were no inspections when we entered here. Thank you for all the women that will meet you here in these pages.'...
>
> 'Thank you, Lord, for the fleas and for...'
>
> The fleas! This was too much! 'Betsie, there is no way that even God can make me thankful for a flea!'
>
> 'Give thanks in *all* circumstances,' she quoted. 'It doesn't say in pleasant circumstances. Fleas are part of this place where God has put us.'
>
> ...We stood between the piers of bunks and gave thanks for the fleas."[19]

Betsie would give away her Bible to someone and another would appear from a sympathetic guard. God's provisions for Corrie and Betsie during terrible circumstances were abundant. Betsie could always see God's Hand of blessing amid the beatings and hardship. That does not mean their time in a prison camp was at all easy. They could have seen only the hardship, but they chose to depend on God and find the blessings and joy within their circumstances. Unfortunately, Corrie was the only one of her family released from Ravensbrúck. Betsie fell ill and died there. Corrie went on to minister to many around the world after World War II.

KEY TO FINDING GOD'S JOY #7:

Believe that God is providing for good to those who love Him. You are never on your own. Turn to God. Choose to see the blessings and find joy.

---

[19] Boom, Corrie Ten with Elizabeth Sherrill and John Sherrill, Copyright © 1971, Grand Rapids, Michigan: Chosen Books (1971) – a division of Baker Publishing Group (1992), p.197-199. All rights restricted. Used by permission of allowance of 250 words.

PRAYERFULLY THINK ABOUT YOUR OWN LIFE WITH GOD:

Are you going through times of happiness or pain right now? Is God making provisions for your situation? What gifts can you find in your circumstances? Sometimes we grow closer to God in these tough times. Sometimes we grow further away in the good times. He wants to know your feelings and needs. God wants to provide for your heart in the midst of good and bad. He loves us!

Sometimes, our circumstances can be so terrible that it is almost impossible to find any provision in the middle of them. If you have lost a young or old child, it is not the way things are to go in life. How can you find any provisions amid that pain? You have to work through your grief and all that comes with it. I do not pretend to understand why that has happened to you. Horrible things happen in this world, and there is no good answer to "Why me, Lord?" God's provisions for you may be there, however. Do you have friends praying for you? Do you have people who are grieving with you? Can you find the strength through the Holy Spirit to be with and help your other children or relatives through this disaster in your life? Can you find the strength through the Holy Spirit to even get up in the morning? There are no easy answers to this. It is one step at a time with the Holy Spirit to guide you. But I do know that God wants to provide for you in your worst times of life.

Maybe there is another type of disaster in your life where you need God's provisions. Like Betsie and Corrie Ten Boom, are you able to be thankful to God in *all* circumstances - almost impossible as it may seem? Ask the Holy Spirit to pray for you. God knows your pain. When my mom was very ill and couldn't seem to get prayers out, I told her to just say, "God, you know." If you need provisions for your life, you can write about them here. Looking back at your life, do you have an example of when God provided for you during your need? Sometimes we see God's provisions for us only after we have worked through the problem with His help. He is your answer through your storms. If you choose to do so, show your thankfulness here. Let God know your appreciation for small or large provisions in your life.

_____

_____

_____

_____

_____

_____

_____

_____

_____

_____

_____

_____

_____

_____

_____

_____

_____

_____

A Song of God's Restoration

My sins were washed away
And my night was turned to day.[20]
- John W. Peterson

*H*ave you ever felt that your life was shattered and that it was now a life with no value to God or others anymore?

I was 24 and in physically weak health after my car accident which almost took my life. I met a man whom I believed would be a good husband for me. He had moved into a house with a couple of Andy's friends from high school, Jack and Kit, who had come to know the Lord. I called to talk to Kit one day, and a strange voice answered the phone. We talked for a while, joking over the phone, and he asked me out for a date. (I will call him Sam.) Sam did make me laugh, and he professed to be a new Christian. This man showered me with gifts as we dated. Within six months, Sam sold his motorcycle to buy an engagement ring for me. My friends were getting married, and it seemed like the right time for me.

---

[20] Peterson, John W., Copyright © 1961, "Heaven Came Down and Glory Filled My Soul", Scottsdale, Arizona: John W. Peterson Music Company, (Renewed 1989). All rights reserved. Used by permission.

Perhaps there were hints that this was not a good match, and I discounted them. Barb's sister, Linda, told me, "Jack and Kit said it is very difficult to live with Sam. He has a temper."

I had never seen that temper. I said, "Whom am I supposed to believe? My future husband or the two guys that may just not like Sam?"

One time I did see a grumpiness. Our entire Berg family had gone to Minneapolis, MN to attend my Grandma Berg's 80th birthday party. I introduced him to all the Bergs, and all seemed to go well. In the evening, my cousins from my mom's side of the family wanted to meet and get to know him. "Do we need to go?" he asked.

"I'd love to see these cousins while we are here. How often are we in Minneapolis?" We rode with a cousin and her husband to meet others, and Sam was quiet and moody.

When I met Sam's mother, I noticed that they fought and yelled a lot. This was so out of my realm of experience, because my family did not fight like this. Maybe because Sam was working for the same company as my dad, I subconsciously thought he might be like my dad. Not physically 100% healthy, I think I chose to fall into my old patterns from before I met the Lord, and I did not dive deeply into myself to see what I was truly feeling or thinking. I'm not sure I even asked God about it. Can you see here that even someone who has miraculously accepted that Jesus is their Lord can completely fall by the wayside and not talk to God or listen to Him about something so important? We all sin. As a couple, Sam and I did not dig deeply into exploring what we expected of marriage.

The man who had been so good to me before marriage said on our wedding night, "You're ugly." This was not the man I had thought I was marrying.

Sam and I attended a seminar at McCormick Place Convention Center in Chicago in the first year of our marriage. The preacher gave teachings on how to put your faith in God, and most of what he said made so much sense. He described a new Christian as a lump of coal. It is pressure from the earth that forms a diamond from coal. Through life's pressures, difficulties, and learning, God molds you closer to His image as you depend on Him. God makes you shine like a diamond.. reflecting His light in the world. The leader also said that you should never divorce for any reason. All differences could be worked out if both partners put their trust in God. I questioned that at the time. What if someone was being beaten?

For five long years, remembering these words about divorce and wanting to protect the diamond I was becoming, I cried every night. We together could not seem to communicate on any topic even as simple as what tile to pick for the kitchen floor. I take some of the blame for this. We were never on the same wavelength as we talked. I was rejected as a partner and ignored often.

When what I wanted to do was not what he wanted, I felt diminished. One time we were in New York City with his best friends. They gave us choices of where we would like to go for the short time we had before we went to dinner.

"I vote for the tour of the NBC studios," I said. Sam reacted with displeasure, but his friends who hardly knew me wanted to please me. Throughout the entire tour, my husband walked at least fifteen feet behind the three of us. I felt embarrassed and tried to carry on the conversation with his friends.

Each night, I cringed when he came home. Sam's temper got out of hand, and I found myself dodging broken glass or plaster of whatever he hit. I worried it was only a matter of time before I would be the receiver of his fists. I pretended that I did not smell the marijuana he was smoking in the basement, since it seemed to help Sam calm down. I yearned to leave. The sparkle to my diamond seemed to be gone.

I could no longer pray. I was confused that this could happen, but I believe I was depressed. I couldn't share my faith, because I thought I was not depending on God and could not have answers for anyone. Worst of all, I did not feel thankful for anything. All seemed dark. I went for a meeting with our pastor. I didn't dare tell him of the problems that I was having at home. I simply told him that I was depressed and that I couldn't pray. I am not even certain whether or not in my mind I tied my home circumstances to my depression. I was numb.

"Why don't we pray about what you are thankful for today?" asked Pastor Cal.

After a long silence and consideration, I said, "I'm not thankful for anything!"

"But you must have something in your life you are thankful for. Think about it, Susan. There is something."

I was living in the darkness of depression, and there was nothingness. Only a long five years of belittlement, fear, and sadness filled my heart. Where had God gone in my life that I had nothing to thank Him for on this day? Finally, it came to me. Barb had been telling me about a book she had been reading about Eskimo women. She had described in detail how the women lived in cold igloos and wore the same clothes for days. They butchered whales after the men caught them and lived with the blood from the butchering on their clothes. I blurted out, "Dear Lord. I'm thankful I'm not an Eskimo woman!"

Hearing myself say that I started to laugh. Pastor Cal started to laugh. My prison and shackles of sadness and depression opened a bit, and I began to pray. With Cal's arm around my shoulder, I thanked God for my parents and brother who loved me, my friend, Barb, who always stood by me, and our church and friends there. I praised God for His goodness in lifting my despair into giggles and thankfulness. There was a pause and for the 2nd and last time in my life thus far, the Holy Spirit prayed for me. I was given the spiritual gift of tongues as words, unrecognizable, poured from my heart. Pastor Cal, who had never heard the gift of tongues, hugged me tightly as I believe the Holy Spirit prayed to God through and for me. We then both sat in silence, awe, and tears. God had begun the work of releasing me from my chains and perhaps bringing a bit of shine back to my diamond.

Later, Sam and I went for counseling together. "You choose the counselor," I said as I didn't want him to have any excuse not to listen to the counselor.

I did not see hope for a happy life together. But could I leave? Would the change be more than I could handle, leaving me with guilt? There was great angst in thinking about moving out on my own and being single again. Most of all, I felt I would be disappointing God whom I loved and chose to serve. After one of our sessions when we were not making any progress, our counselor suggested that we come individually. I spent time looking at my part in the difficulties we were having. I did not always let Sam know how I was feeling. I stuffed down anger or hurt rather than talking about it. I lived in fear all the time, not knowing how he would react to the slightest thing. Sam never did hit me. The counselor was not surprised or in disagreement, however, when I requested a divorce. This was a big decision for me, and the pain of it all was terrible. How could I be getting a divorce when I had vowed my life to this man in front of God?

I moved out to live with my friend, Andy, and his new wife, Gwen, for several months at the PTL (Praise the Lord) House belonging to 1st Presbyterian in Aurora. Andy was ministering to singles there.

I eventually moved to a new apartment of my own, but the failure I felt would not lift. Divorce should not have been an option, but I believe I had no choice. I had let the hammer come down on my diamond. I know that the diamond is the hardest stone in the world and would be impossible to crush. However, every night, I would pray that God would restore me and give me peace. In my mind, I would imagine the diamond I was becoming now shattered on the floor. Every night!!!

"God, I can no longer reflect Your light to others. My diamond is shattered! Forgive me, Lord." Each night was the same. I had failed to become all God wanted me to be. I could not share with others anymore.

Our God is great! He did not want me to go on feeling closed off from other people. In Him, I could be renewed and made whole. One night, as I "saw" my diamond in pieces on the floor, I prayed again that God would heal me. In my soul I heard, *"Susan. Yes. Your diamond is shattered. But I can take all of those pieces and put them back together into the most beautiful setting you have ever seen."* I knew at that moment that my inability to see and share my blessings and all of my heartbreak were washed away. God was seeing the beauty in His creation of me and restoring me. Peace! Joy! It was like the words of John W. Peterson's hymn, *Heaven Came Down, and Glory Filled My Soul.*

*Heaven came down, and Glory filled my soul. When at
the cross, the Savior made me whole.*[21]

I felt whole again. I never looked back. God was in the process of
resetting my diamond.

~~~~~~~~~~~~~~~~~~~~~~~~~~~~~~~~~~~~~

LET'S TALK ABOUT GOD'S RESTORATION:

Have you ever needed the restoration that God can provide? There
are many reasons why we may need that restoration, bringing you
back to your peace and joy and your close relationship with the Lord.
Perhaps you have been in a situation like mine where there was no
good solution to your marriage, and you needed to get a divorce. It
is very hard to reconcile that in your heart. You may feel broken.
God can restore your heart and give you peace and joy again. Give
it to Him. I pray that God has restored Sam and has given him a life
that God meant him to live in God's peace!

Another example of the need for restoration: As Christians, we are
still in the world and sinful. I still sin. I do not want to sin, but I do
at times. Perhaps I spend too much money on myself only thinking
of my wants. Maybe I get envious of what another has. Sometimes,
I have a hard time forgiving. I also struggle with worry which means
I am not trusting God. Sometimes I commit the sin of omission in
that I see a need, and I just do not act in the way God would want
me to act. Yet our sins have been washed away by the blood of Jesus
as He died for us, and we accepted Him as our Savior. If we are
walking with the Lord, we ask forgiveness for our sins on a regular
basis knowing that Jesus has already died to make us clean and

---

worthy of being in His kingdom. Then we go on, letting the light of God shine through us. Restoration!

A third example of the need for restoration has to do with ego. If our ego is getting in the way of our relationship with God or others, we need restoration. We can get all puffed up with what wonderful Christians we are and how we have done so much for God.

Oswald Chambers said it very well. "It's one thing to go through a crisis grandly, yet quite another to go through every day glorifying God when there is no witness, no limelight, and no one paying even the remotest attention to us. If we are not looking for halos, we at least want something that will make people say, 'What a wonderful man of prayer he is!' or 'What a great woman of devotion she is.' If you are properly devoted to the Lord Jesus, you have reached the lofty height where no one would ever notice you personally. All that is noticed is the power of God coming through you all the time... We tend to set up success in Christian work as our purpose, but our purpose should be to display the glory of God in human life, to live a life 'hidden with Christ in God in our everyday human conditions' (Colossians 3:3). Our human relationships are the very conditions in which the ideal life of God should be exhibited."[22]

One time at 1st Presbyterian Church in Aurora, IL, our church was honoring a former pastor-evangelist, Peter Joshua. Mrs. Billy Graham, whom Pastor Joshua had influenced, spoke. Then Mrs. Peter Joshua went to the pulpit. She told of a time when she was speaking at a church and inside of the pulpit there was a sign: It read, "Sir: We would see Jesus". How important it is when one is sharing about the Lord and even writing a book about Him that we totally

---

[22] Taken from *My Utmost for His Highest* by Oswald Chambers, edited by James Reimann, © 1992 by Oswald Chambers Publications Assn., Ltd., "Still Human!" Entry November 16, and used by permission of Our Daily Bread Publishing, Grand Rapids MI 49501. All rights reserved.

depend on Him. I pray, as you continue to read my book, that you will see God, not Susan. This is HIS story.

Some who do not know the Lord may see our sins or our ego and call us hypocrites. But no one is perfect. Only Jesus was perfect. Some do not see their own sin and need the restoration that God can bring. Some feel guilty about their sin, thinking God can never forgive them. But the truth is that I have been told the Bible speaks way more about how much God loves us than about how we should love him. God loves us! He wants His best for us. In the Bible I read:

> And the God of all grace, who called you to His eternal glory in Christ, after you have suffered a little while, will Himself restore you and make you strong, firm, and steadfast.
>
> **1 Peter 5:10 (NIV)**

Even the great King David of the Bible committed terrible sins. His ego was a big part of it. After he committed adultery with Bathsheba, he wrote in the Psalms:

> Have mercy on me, O God, according to Your unfailing love; according to Your great compassion blot out my transgressions. Wash away all my iniquity and cleanse me from my sin.
>
> **Psalm 51:1-2 (NIV)**

And he continues:

> Do not cast me from Your presence or take Your Holy Spirit from me. Restore to me the joy of Your salvation and grant me a willing spirit, to sustain me.
>
> **Psalm 51:11-12 (NIV)**

God did restore the joy in David and through David, God brought about good. It was the line of David's descendants that brought us the Messiah, Jesus Christ. Now that is true restoration when all seems bleak in the world. David was not always a good man. God restored His relationship with David and brought about the greatest gift the world has ever known.

KEY TO FINDING GOD'S JOY #8:

If you have given your heart to Jesus, He is <u>always</u> there with you. If you need restoration for any reason, go to Him. Then let your restoration point to the Lord and give you joy. If you have sinned or let your ego get in the way, you need restoration. Ask forgiveness and be loved and restored into your relationship with Jesus. He loves you!

PRAYERFULLY THINK ABOUT YOUR OWN LIFE WITH GOD:

Have you experienced restoration from the Lord? Has an experience in your life made you feel like a failure? What was that? God can restore you. Is there anything in your life separating you from the love of your God who is there? Perhaps you need restoration through repentance. Maybe you have never thought about your sin and have not asked God to forgive and restore you. Has something else in your life become your god, such as money, prestige, shopping, popularity, intellectualism, etc.? All of these do not bring you peace and joy with God. Ego!

Are you trying to buy your way or make yourself important enough to find your way to Heaven? Remember that Jesus said that blessed are the meek for they shall inherit the earth. Restoration is also about being restored to the Kingdom of God here on earth, not just thinking about what will happen after you die. It is about loving others more than ourselves. Being restored will give you peace and joy now. What are your thoughts after you have read about the reasons we can need God's restoration? What will you do if you need restoration?

_____

_____

_____

_____

_____

_____

_____

_____

_____

_____

_____

_____

_____

_____

_____

_____

_____

_____

A Song of God's Model

Jesus loves the little children of the world.
- C. Herbert Woolston and George F. Root

I moved forward after my divorce with the assurance that Jesus was with me. I was given strength by reading Paul's letter to the Philippians:

> being confident of this, that He who began a good work in you will carry it on to completion until the day of Christ Jesus.
>
> **Philippians 1:6 (NIV)**

This imperfect follower of Jesus clung to the idea that He would continue to teach me and change me, to polish my diamond in the way I should become.

While still married to my husband, I had started my Master of Science degree in Special Education with specialties in Teaching Children with Learning Disabilities and also Teaching Children with Behavior Disorders. I had been teaching 2nd or 3rd graders for 8 years. After receiving my master's degree, I taught learning disabilities for one year and then began my calling to teach children with behavior disorders. I say "my calling", because not many

teachers gravitate to a roomful of troubled kids! I had the youngest
- the kindergarten through 3rd graders who loved to tantrum. They
also had the distinction of being children who usually chose to do
the opposite of what a teacher asked them to do. I was supposed to
have no more than 8 children with an aide. However, the school
district petitioned the state to "allow" me to have 13 in my room. I
taught these dear children with what God was using to teach me -
love, boundaries, and consistency. How God taught me was my
model for teaching my students. My teaching life brings to mind the
song, *Jesus Loves the Little Children.*

> *Jesus loves the little children, all the children of the*
> *world.*
> *Red and yellow, black and white; all are precious in His*
> *sight.*
> *Jesus loves the little children of the world.*[23]

I loved every one of my kids. After our first few weeks of tumult, I
think they loved me too.

"Dear Heavenly Father. Be with me to help my students to progress
in their learning as well as to control their behaviors. Give me
wisdom, kindness, patience, and understanding just as You have
shown to me," I prayed each day.

Certain children who always refused to do something such as line
up were miraculously compliant with my request when I worded it,
"You <u>probably don't</u> want to line up right now." The wording
confused them, and they thought they were doing the opposite of

---

[23] Woolston, Clare Herbert (words), Copyright thought to be sometime in the late 1800's, "Jesus
Loves the Little Children", in the Public Domain, George F. Root (music), Copyright © 1864,
originally the tune "Tramp Tramp Tramp" set to the words of "Jesus Loves the Little Children", in
the Public Domain..

what I was asking by lining up. They eventually figured out the trick!

But God did not want me to have to use tricks. I know He wanted a complete change for these children in how they reacted to authority and how they grew and learned. I sensed the best way to teach was for my kids to experience complete love from me. Many times in their homes, they were not feeling loved. What had brought them to my room was different for each child. I had to depend on God for answers to the needs of all my children. Some succeeded in rejoining regular classrooms. Some did not. I wasn't at all sure that the way I was teaching through relationship and love was best for the kids. Of course, it was good in that they had good years of learning while with me. However, their relationship with me did not always transfer out of the classroom to other environments.

During one trip to Brookfield Zoo near Chicago, I had recruited enough teachers to go with us along with my aide, Jane, and her husband, Dick. Each adult was responsible and had the hands of two children. All was going well until one of the boys needed to use the bathroom. Dick took all the boys into the bathroom. He looked on in amazement. The boys immediately began to scale the walls of the toilet stalls and crawl up on the sinks. Two big men walked in and immediately turned around and left. Dick told me he said to himself, "If those big guys don't dare come in, what am I doing here?!" He left to find me. The control I had in the classroom didn't quite transfer to Dick that day.

Some of my students on this day at Brookfield Zoo piled on
as I sat on the curb. What joy! We loved each other!

At the end of 4 years, I asked our principal, "Do you think you could find a Behavior Disorders teacher for next year? I need a breather from the stress, and I'd like to go back to a regular classroom."

"Oh, Susan. It's really hard to find teachers of children with behavior disorders. The district won't let you have a break in a regular classroom. Maybe you should put out your resume to our neighbors to the east in Naperville." This was very kind of him considering that he was the principal who was going to have to find a new BD teacher.

What a blessing it was to have the privilege of teaching my children with behavior disorders for four years. Sometimes, seeing what was going on in their lives made any problem I had seem mild. Oh, how I loved and prayed for them. I have been in contact with a few who are in their late forties now. One is agonizing over her life, and she needs our prayers. One would stick his foot out all the time to trip my aide in my classroom but had a smile that could melt your heart. He was just baptized and became a Christian this past year. God be with all of my former students.

I left Aurora to teach 3rd grade in Naperville, Illinois. I was blessed with the greatest principal a teacher could ever have. She taught all of her teachers how to become better for the kids. Mary Anne had a gift and passed that gift from God onto me. The years that followed at two different schools with her were full of hard work but joy! Blessings came in the form of wonderful teammates, a small group of teachers who prayed together after school for their students and their own children, a fantastic group of supportive parents, and new wonderful friends who prayed for me.

All 3rd graders in my care were new puzzles from God to decipher as to how to best teach them. I loved them! I used again what God was using to teach me. He was my teaching model. Once again, to all, I needed to show love, boundaries, and consistency.

At the beginning of each school year, I asked my 3rd graders what they had heard about me. For some crazy reason, the same words always emerged. I was strict, kind, and fun! I am rather happy with those descriptors.

Let me tell you about 3rd graders. They are wonderful and excited about all things new. They can learn more in one year than they have in the previous 3 years. One negative is that they usually begin to feel peer pressure in 3rd grade. In 1st and 2nd grade, children are normally more aware of their teachers and parents. All of a sudden in 3rd, they realize that some kids are getting more attention than others. Some are more "popular". Their peers become their focus, but they don't know how to become popular with their peers. Some poke at others or make fun of others to make themselves feel better. Others become class clowns. Some try to separate some of the students from others, a power play.

Remember. I was trying to teach as God was teaching me with love, boundaries, consistency, and sometimes discipline. There was a little girl in one class of 3rd graders who was smart and sweet. She was a natural leader. (I have asked Allie's permission to share her story.) Allie realized that groups were forming in the classroom, and as a leader, she began whispering to other girls to not play with certain girls. It was time for an intervention. I asked Allie to stay in at recess one day for a talk.

"Allie, what is going on with you and the other girls? Everyone seems to be leaving some girls out of their groups."

"I don't know, Mrs. Heeg. We just like to play with certain girls. Do we have to play with everyone?"

"Let me put it this way. How would you feel if some of the girls left you out of their group all of the time? Allie, you are a strong leader. That is a powerful position to be in when you are young. As I see it, you can be a negative leader and pull girls apart from each other or you can be a positive leader and work to have all the girls respect each other and not leave others out. That doesn't mean you can't have best friends. Which do you think you want to be?"

"I think I want to try to be a strong positive leader," said Allie.

"Oh, I was hoping that you would use your power for good, Allie. Now go out and have fun!"

Allie turned it around in 3rd grade. There weren't any more problems with groups forming and hurting the feelings of those left out of the group. In fifth grade, Allie was presented the Citizenship Award out of the 120 students in the 5th-grade classes.

After the awards assembly, Allie's mom came to my room. She told me she had asked Allie how out of all those kids, she was the one who received the Citizenship Award. Her mom said she just really wanted me to know Allie's answer. She had told her mom that back in 3rd grade, Mrs. Heeg had kept her in at recess and had talked to her about how she could be a negative or a positive leader. She had chosen that day to become a positive leader, bringing kids together. I cried at this news. God's model had worked beautifully. It always does.

I got the joy of attending Allie's wedding, and she and Jack now have a baby boy. I am sure that she is still a positive leader in all she does. What a blessing!

Of course, with my behavior disorders background, I always seemed to find that the one child who was struggling the most with behavior was in my 3rd-grade classroom. Allie was not one of these! (Don't tell any of my other students, but that one having the most behavioral difficulties always had a special place in my heart.) So many others did too, and I am still blessed to be in contact through Facebook, Instagram, email, or cards with many former students. They make me so proud to know them. I am even in contact with several from my very first class in 1971. Some are grandparents now! What a blessing to love your job and to see the results of your hard work! I am thankful for God's model in my teaching! I retired with 34 years of joyous teaching behind me.

~~~~~~~~~~~~~~~~~~~~~~~~~~~~~~

LET'S TALK ABOUT GOD'S MODEL:

In teaching, it was so important to help each child feel cared about and competent to conquer any learning or behavior. This is truly "What would Jesus do?" Jesus loved the little children so much that when the disciples were arguing about which of them was the greatest, He stopped them from doing so:

> Jesus, knowing their thoughts, took a little child and had him stand beside Him. Then He said to them, "Whoever welcomes this little child in My name welcomes Me, and whoever welcomes Me welcomes the One who sent Me. For it is the one who is least among you all who is the greatest."
>
> **Luke 9:47- 48 (NIV)**

Children were the greatest in Jesus' eyes. I believe this is because they see things simply. Jesus said to come unto Him as little children. It is simple obedience in faith that brings us to the point of accepting the truth of the Lord Jesus Christ. It is not with in-depth analysis.

That doesn't mean God doesn't want us to ask questions. I used to ask my students, "Do you think there are people smarter than you in our class?" Many thought so. Then, I would ask them, "How do you think those kids got that smart? Do you think they magically knew all the answers before others?" The kids guessed, but I always needed to point out that "Smart kids ask questions. That is how they get smart." We come to knowledge and faith in Jesus like that of a little child. One step toward him, giving him your full attention and love, brings you to the heart of God and God's song in your soul. Then, we gain God's wisdom and knowledge as we study, ask questions, and let the Holy Spirit work to transform us.

How important it is in all our days of work and life to honor God and let him be our model for our reactions during our time here on earth. Pray every day for good outcomes with relationships and events at your job and in all of your life.

KEY TO FINDING GOD'S JOY #9:

Let God be your model in all you do in friendships, in relations with strangers, and in your job. Find a job in your life that you love. If you can't do that, find love for your job. Ask God to help you find the good in your employment or pray that God will help you find a new job. Each day, come to Jesus as a little child, simply accepting his love and goodness and passing that on to your coworkers and all whom you know. In all your relationships, think of the old saying, "What would Jesus do?" Then carry on in that manner. This will give you joy.

PRAYERFULLY THINK ABOUT YOUR OWN LIFE WITH GOD:

How do you feel about your job? One way we show others that Jesus is love is by loving others as Jesus loves us. If we can't do that on our job and in life or forgive the mistakes of others, we are not being the Christians whom Jesus teaches us to be. We are not following his model. Of course, that does not mean that we do not help others correct their mistakes in a kind way. That is important in any job.

How do you get along with your fellow employees? If the answer is poorly, what can you do about that? Your job is a very important part of your life. It takes up much of your time. Let Jesus help you have the best work experience possible. What can you do to allow the Lord to help you in your work situation? If you love your job, praise God for this blessing. Reflect on God's model in all facets of your life. Are you considering what Jesus would do as a model for you whenever you are making decisions about job, family, friends, or situations? Reflect on God's model in your work life and all other situations.

_____

_____

_____

_____

_____

_____

_____

_____

_____

_____

_____

_____

_____

_____

_____

_____

_____

_____

_____

10
A Song of God's Strength

The Lord has promised good to me,
His Word my hope secures.
- John Newton

After reading about my divorce, you may be curious to know what was going on in my private life. After I moved into my own apartment, I concentrated on my job and God and the peace He finally gave me over getting a divorce. God was at work for the good in my life, and I didn't know it.

One night the next year, I was out for a walk in the courtyard of my apartment complex. I heard a voice call from the 2nd-floor balcony of my building. "Hi, there! I think we have a mutual friend."

As I looked up, I saw a very handsome man leaning on the railing. He smiled and I asked, "Whom would that be?"

"Barb. I know her through her dad, Keith, and the group of men who built the Hilton Inn. When she came to visit you the other day, we passed in the doorway to the building. I asked her whom she was coming to see, and she told me it was her friend Sue on the first floor. Do you want to come up and talk for a while? I'm David, by the way."

I did take him up on his offer and that began a marathon of talking that went on for months. David was a divorced father of two boys, David Jr. and Jason. They were in elementary and junior high school at the time. David did not go to church but had attended just one of our Bible studies through friendship with Barb. He had been raised in the church, and very often our conversations were about the Lord. He was seeking.

David was an air traffic controller and loved his job. It was hard to see each other, because I worked from 8 a.m. to all hours of the evening grading papers and planning. He worked the 2 p.m. to 10 p.m. shift at the Aurora air traffic center. Often, our talks were late at night after he returned home. David had been greatly hurt in his divorce, and he truly felt he would never be able to love again. I, on the other hand, was falling for this man. His wit was unsurpassed. I ended up laughing all of the time in our conversations. He was always so kind to me! We managed to get in a dinner at our favorite Mexican restaurant once in a while, but for the most part, we sat on the balcony or in the living room and talked… sometimes all night on a weekend. I didn't know if we were just good friends, or if we were developing a romantic relationship. There were some very good kisses along the way, however!!

"Hey. Come over here, guys. I want you to meet someone," David yelled to his boys who were diving into the pool at our complex. They came scurrying over, dripping wet. "This is my friend, Susan, and this is David Jr. and Jason."

"I'm glad to meet you," I said. "I've heard about how great you are from your dad."

Jason was in Little League, and I attended a game. David Jr. went to our church camp in Wisconsin when I was there, and often he liked to spend time talking with me at the beach. He was as witty as his dad. We had all begun a good relationship.

Then in 1981 David was involved with the air traffic controllers' strike over outdated equipment amongst other issues. David and the boys picketed, but in the end, President Reagan fired all of the strikers. The president had promised the controllers before the election that he would make sure all of their equipment was updated. Now David found himself out of a job.

David told me, "Sometimes the screens in front of me showing planes in the air just go blank. I lose track of the planes I'm tracking. I call maintenance, but they usually just bang on the screen, and the planes are back." New equipment was the big safety issue the men and women were fighting for in this strike. Of course, there were other issues of pay and insurance. Before the election, President Reagan had seemed like he was the only one in their corner when he spoke with the union. They had all voted for him, and now they were fired. David was angry and didn't know what he would do now to find other employment..

Without my knowing, David went to a Christian revival meeting. He came home a changed man.

"I asked Jesus to come into my heart. I actually forgave President Reagan," he said. God brought the most important life-changing good for David out of this tough time in his life. What a blessing! In the words of David's favorite hymn, *Amazing Grace*, we see the praise he felt in his soul.

> *Amazing Grace, how sweet the sound that saved a wretch like me.*
> *I once was lost but now I'm found. Was blind but now I see.* [24]

---

[24] Newton, John, Copyright © 1779, "Amazing Grace", in the Public Domain. Music 1st linked in 1835 to unknown author of the folksong "New Britain" in the Public Domain.

Now, David needed to find a job that he could enjoy. He was sad at having lost the job he loved. He told me, "I'm willing to sweep floors and clean toilets as long as I don't have to do it in front of my friends here in Aurora."

On Easter night, we talked. "Let's turn off the stereo," David said. I knew it was important. "I've been offered a job by my friend, Jim, to study and then manage an insurance agency in Kingman, Arizona. I told him I would take it." We were not in a committed place for me to go with him. David and I would be ending our relationship. Tears filled my eyes and my heart ached.

On the night before he was leaving with his loaded trailer, we sat on the floor in his empty apartment all night and talked, laughed, held hands, and both cried. "You'll need to find a church when you get to Kingman. I'll be praying for you," I said. "I'm just going to ask one thing of you. Please don't ever call me. This is going to be very hard, because you know I love you."

That next morning, tears just flowed as I watched him pull out of the courtyard, never to be seen again. It was one of the most painful days of my life.

I called Barb, and we met down by the river at a park. I couldn't stop crying, but I knew I had to move on and find strength in the Lord. We prayed together and decided that I needed a tangible symbol that David was truly gone. The strength of the Lord would get me through this time.

"I know," I said. "I'm moving into David's old apartment because there are two bedrooms. He left those beds with the navy bedding in the boys' room for me. Those beds are never going to have little boys sleeping in them again. If I change the bedding to something very 'girlie', I will force myself to realize that my time with David and the boys is over." God would get me through this. The next day, the beds were fitted with lovely floral comforters!

~~~~~~~~~~~~~~~~~~~~~~~~~~~~~~~~~~~~

LET'S TALK ABOUT GOD'S STRENGTH:

I realize that life does not always wrap up into a neat little package. What is it that we truly value that we call blessings? In this part of my life that you just read, I found my strength in realizing the greatest blessing was that David found Jesus amid the pain in his life. He also learned to forgive. Redemption in Jesus was a far greater blessing than the possibility of my engagement and marriage to the man I loved. I could find joy in that. If David had never surrendered his life to Christ, I wouldn't have been able to marry him anyway. We wouldn't have understood life and God's will for us in the same way.

God is not a blessings "vending machine" that doles out blessings of our choice when we pray. Yes, we recognize when the great blessings come. But life doesn't always work like that. Sometimes, God's blessing is peace amid the pain in our lives and a new direction.

Notice in this Psalm:

> The Lord gives strength to His people; The Lord blesses
> His people with peace.
>
> **Psalms 29:11 (NIV)**

The Lord God gives strength and peace. God gave me the strength to realize that David was not coming back. He helped me to move on and to rest in His strong arms.

I like what Oswald Chambers has to say about strength. "God does not give us overcoming life - He gives us life as we overcome. The strain of life is what builds our strength. If there is no strain, there will be no strength. Are you asking God to give you life, liberty, and joy? He cannot unless you are willing to accept the strain. And once you face the strain, you will immediately get the strength."[25]

I once heard of a very good professional baseball pitcher who had done so well at first that the pressure in each game became unbearable. He had tried many self-help programs. He wasn't a strong pitcher anymore. It wasn't until he realized that Jesus took him just as he was, that he knew he didn't have to be perfect in every way. He could depend on the Lord for his peace and his strength, so he accepted Jesus as Lord. He found joy in his life again. He faced the strain through the Lord's help and received strength to carry on in his life.

> So do not fear, for I am with you; do not be dismayed,
> for I am your God. I will strengthen you and help you.
> I will uphold you with My righteous right hand.
> **Isaiah 41:10 (NIV)**

KEY TO FINDING GOD'S JOY #10:

When disappointment overtakes you and you have lost hope, know that God's strength will support you. When the stress of life is at its worst, God builds strength in his people when you give it to Him. Asking for God's strength will bring you to joy and peace once again, deep in your heart.

---

[25] Taken from *My Utmost for His Highest* by Oswald Chambers, edited by James Reimann, © 1992 by Oswald Chambers Publications Assn., Ltd., "The Teaching of Adversity", Entry August 2, and used by permission of Our Daily Bread Publishing, Grand Rapids MI 49501. All rights reserved.

PRAYERFULLY THINK ABOUT YOUR OWN LIFE WITH GOD:

Is it possible to be thankful for the stress in our lives that brings us closer to God? If you are flying through life with no tough times, you are unique. Some people have worse difficult times than others, but we all experience the strain that can bring us back to God for his strength. Do you have a time now when you feel disappointment or stress that has overwhelmed you? What happened? Have you turned to God for strength or are you trying to solve it on your own? In the past, have you come through a tough time through the strength of God? Take a few moments to think about God's strength leading you through those tough times to a joy deep in your heart knowing you have peace in your struggle. If you are one of the fortunate ones to have not faced stressful times, how can you prepare yourself for when those times come?

_____

_____

_____

_____

_____

_____

_____

_____

_____

_____

_____

_____

A Song of
God's Blessings

Perfect submission all is at rest
I in my Savior am happy and blest
- Fanny Crosby and Phoebe Palmer Knapp

$\mathcal{W}$hen we submit to the will of God and rest in His arms, sometimes He brings us to the end of the pain and once again we learn. Much of the summer passed, and the phone rang.

"Hi, Susan. This is David. I know you said not to call, but I miss you so much. What would you think about coming to Arizona for a visit.?" Absence does make the heart grow fonder. With much hesitation, I agreed.

David ran to me when he picked me up at the airport in Las Vegas. Our hug was full of electricity! On the way to Kingman, Arizona where he lived, we stopped for lunch at a little place on the way which was an old-time town called Old Vegas. There was a singer in the restaurant who sounded just like Willie Nelson. My mind floats back to the song, "Always on My Mind"[26] made famous by Willie Nelson which we heard that day. David had always been on my mind. It was a fight every day to keep him out of my mind. We

---

[26] Carson, Wayne with Johnny Christopher and Mark James, Copyright © 1982, "Always on My Mind". Columbia Records, Sony Corporation: New York City, NY.

crossed the Hoover Dam on our way to Kingman and parked and explored. The day was full of joy!

Kingman was an average-sized town in northwestern Arizona. There were sandstorms and big winds all the time in that desert community. Everything was brown, and it was a stark contrast to the lush green summers of Aurora, Illinois. David and I had so much fun visiting the London Bridge. My favorite activity was climbing mountains and seeing beautiful desert sunsets together. We had many serious talks during this time.

The best? "I love you, Susan," David told me at the top of a mountain as the sun was setting! There was not a big proposal. "What do you think?" asked David. "Should we get married?"

"Oh yes!"

I hugged him with all my strength. We were such good friends that we just easily talked about everything. We decided that I would quit my job at the winter semester break and move to Arizona.

This was not God's plan, however. The boys had gone to Arizona to see their dad earlier in the summer, and David missed them terribly when they left. They were now living full-time with their mom in Aurora, whereas before David moved, the boys split their time between their mom and their dad. David called me after I returned to Aurora to tell me that he was going to organize things in the business in Kingman, and he would be quitting and returning to Illinois in mid-October. We set a date to get married in October of 1982.

David also let the boys know he was returning and that we were getting married. They were so excited that their dad was coming home! David Jr., Jason, and I got to know each other even better.

They came to swim in our apartment pool, played on my mini-trampoline, threw the ball around in the courtyard, and attended a church fair with me at 1st Presbyterian Church. The boys seemed excited that their dad was marrying me. We had established a good relationship. My situation with the boys couldn't have been better. Another great blessing! From the hymn, *Blessed Assurance*:

> *This is my story, this is my song; Praising my Savior all the day long.*
> *This is my story, this is my song; Praising my Savior all the day long.*[27]

David Jr. and Jason attend the 1st Presbyterian Fun Fair with me while we wait for Dad to come home.

---

[27] Crosby, Fanny Jane (Words) Copyright © 1876 and Phoebe Palmer Knapp (Music) Copyright © 1876, "Blessed Assurance", in the Public Domain.

In late August on the night before school would start in Aurora, I had friends over for dinner.

"AAAAA!" I screamed. I was poking the baking potatoes with a knife to break the skin. It happened so quickly. I don't recall poking a softer potato or seeing my hand slide down the knife and the knife slice through my pinkie finger to the bone. My friends rushed me to the emergency room for stitches on the finger that wouldn't stop bleeding.

The doctor who examined me had bad news. "The tendon is cut to the bone and has snapped clear up into your wrist. You need major surgery to repair the tendon on that right pinkie, and then you will have a cast up to your elbow to steady the repair."

With school starting the next day, I had to leave my new behavior disorders class with a poor substitute teacher for the first week of school. Close your eyes and imagine the horror stories of children riding their desks around the room, fights, and tantrums!

I returned to a classroom after a week where I had to lay down the law. I took each child into the hall to show them where their place would be to hang their coats and leave their lunches. As I did so, I had a special message for each of them about what I had heard of their behaviors during the first week of school. For the one little guy who had just ridden his desk around the room nonstop, I said, "I have a cast on my arm. I will not be able to stop you from doing wrong things, because it might hurt my arm. If you aren't going to behave, I will have to remove you from the classroom and perhaps send you home." This little boy behaved perfectly until the day I got my cast off my arm!!

My cast came off the week before David was to return from Kingman.

In mid-October, David drove nonstop from Arizona to Aurora, Illinois. He knocked on the door before I ever expected him. "David! You're here! I can't believe it! God is so good! We're going to be together!"

"I never stopped except to get gas," he said. "I couldn't wait any longer to see you!"

The reunion between the boys and their dad was also worth every minute of waiting. They hugged him so tightly that I thought he may be squeezed to death!

We planned a quick wedding at the chapel at 1st Presbyterian for the family. The week before the wedding, I dropped the sun tea jar on the floor and shattered the glass. My right hand was weak from having a cast on it for a long time. My fingers bled a bit as I picked up pieces of glass, but there were only a few cuts. Cuts or no cuts, I was ready to get married!

My parents, my brother, and his wife arrived from Michigan. David's mom, sister, brother-in-law, and nephew were in attendance from Aurora. Barb was my matron of honor, and David Jr. and Jason stood up for their dad. The service was very simple. Barb played the piano as David and I walked into the chapel together. The minister began the ceremony.

It came time to exchange rings. The minister began, "Wear these rings as a reminder of the vows you have just taken. Susan, please place the ring on David's finger."

David held out his hand and up and down every finger of his hand, David had placed Band-Aids! I immediately began laughing so hard that I was crying. This was my David.

The minister looked troubled. "Are you all right?" he asked. He didn't know why I was laughing so hard and neither did our family. Only David would joke about all my recent episodes with knives and shards of glass like this on our wedding day. I finally got the ring past his Band-Aids, and we were married!

David had me laughing even after the wedding! What a joyful day!

That is a perfect picture of David. To this day, he says, "Watch out! Susan's in the kitchen with knives!" He has made me laugh every day of our lives together. God's gift to me that day has gotten even better by the day and month and year.

LET'S TALK ABOUT GOD'S BLESSINGS:

I am so thankful for the blessings I have just described. Blessings can come in good or bad times. Sometimes, we get a greater blessing and understanding of the Lord our God by clinging to him in the toughest times of our lives. It was a blessing that David moved away and realized that he did love me. It certainly didn't feel like that at the time of his leaving. It was sheer pain. But in reality, his leaving was a blessing.

Jesus spoke of who receives blessings in the Beatitudes during His Sermon on the Mount:

He said:

> "Blessed are the poor in spirit, for theirs is the kingdom of heaven.
> Blessed are those who mourn, for they will be comforted.
> Blessed are the meek, for they will inherit the earth.
> Blessed are those who hunger and thirst for righteousness, for they will be filled.
> Blessed are the merciful, for they will be shown mercy.
> Blessed are the pure in heart, for they will see God.
> Blessed are the peacemakers, for they will be called children of God.
> Blessed are those who are persecuted because of righteousness, for theirs is the kingdom of heaven.
> Blessed are you when people insult you, persecute you, and falsely say all kinds of evil against you because of me.
> Rejoice and be glad, because great is your reward in heaven, for in the same way they persecuted the prophets who were before you."
>
> **Matthew 5:3-12 (NIV)**

As you can see from those Jesus said were blessed, it is not always easy to be blessed. However, there are promises in the beatitudes which show us that God does bless us with comfort and mercy and fills us with God's righteousness through the power of the Holy Spirit. In really hard times, our rewards are in heaven. Thanks be to God who blesses us in good and tough times.

Billy Graham, in a book called *The Secret of Happiness*, speaks of the joy that only comes through the Lord. "One kind of happiness comes to us when our circumstances are pleasant and we are relatively free from troubles. The problem, however, is that that kind of happiness is fleeting and superficial. When circumstances change – as they inevitably do – then this kind of happiness evaporates like the early morning fog in the heat of the sun... The second kind of happiness is a lasting, inner joy and peace which survives any circumstances. It is a happiness which endures no matter what comes our way – and even may grow stronger in adversity. This is the kind of happiness to which Jesus summons us in the Beatitudes. It is a happiness which can only come from God... The happiness for which our souls ache is one undisturbed by success or failure, one which dwells deep within us and gives inward relaxation, peace, and contentment, no matter what the surface problems may be. That kind of happiness stands in need of no outward stimulus."[28]

Happiness is of the moment. Joy is in the heart and soul. Praise God that this type of joy is available to us through our Lord!

KEY TO FINDING GOD'S JOY #11:

Realize what your blessings truly are and experience the huge blessings along with the small everyday ones that God brings into

---

[28] Graham, Billy, Copyright © 1985, *The Secret of Happiness. Revised and Expanded ed.,* Nashville, Tennessee: Word Books Publishers, pages 18, 19, 20.. All rights reserved. Used by permission.

your life. Realize when hardships could really be blessings and sense the joy which is there deep down in your soul.

PRAYERFULLY THINK ABOUT YOUR OWN LIFE WITH GOD:

Can you list the blessings which God has given you? Have blessings come when you least expected them? If you know Jesus, God is blessing you every day. Sometimes, we just have to stop and take stock of what He has done in our lives.

Have you ever had a terrible hardship turn into a blessing? When was that? Or, perhaps you have had the most terrible hardships such as a loss of a child or rape which can never turn into a blessing. If you helped one other person get through the same trauma as you did, you have blessed that person. God has used you for His good and used your difficult or traumatic experiences for good. That is a blessing. Are you angry with God and do not want to see what He is doing in your life? Maybe you are fortunate enough to see all that God is doing in your life. A journal each day of gratitude to God for His blessings can be a good way to start. Take a few moments to reflect on your blessings.

_____

_____

_____

_____

_____

_____

_____

God's Song of Care

Jesus loves me, this I know.
- Anna B. Warner and William Bradbury

David and I were married when that little guy in my behavior disorders class who rode his desk around the room had decided to act up again. It was a couple of weeks after I got my cast off my arm. David immediately jumped in to help. He said, "Why don't you tell him that if he behaves as well as he did while you had your cast on for say one month, I will write him a letter of congratulations and bring it to school in person."

My class knew that I had just been married. I relayed the offer to the desk rider that day. "I can do it," he said. We made a little chart so that he could count off the days. A month went by with good behavior.

David came to school with the letter and met him as he got off the bus. "I am so proud of you for making it easier on my new wife and for changing your ways. I'm also going to keep an eye out for your future behaviors. You're a good guy!"

The students got into a line to walk through the school to our room. Here he came, as proud as could be, holding the letter high in the air for everyone in the school to notice as we walked by them. I had tears in my eyes to see him so proud and happy. He had a wonderful turn-around at that point. David had cared about him, and it meant a lot. That was the kind of man I had married. This was an answer to prayers for this one little student and for me!

This incident with my student, my love for all my students, and my new relationship with my husband and my stepsons made me want to shout for joy. I had wanted love and family in my life. I had always loved my students. These blessings make me want to sing the simple song from my childhood, *Jesus Loves Me.*

> *Jesus loves me this I know. For the Bible tells me so.*
> *Little ones to Him belong. They are weak but He is*
> *strong.*
> *Yes, Jesus loves me. Yes, Jesus loves me.*
> *Yes, Jesus loves me. The Bible tells me so.*[29]

After our marriage, my relationship with David's sons, David Jr. and Jason, grew even more. David and I had agreed that we would discuss discipline issues between ourselves, but he would always follow through with any discipline needed. I believe that God cared about me and about David and the boys enough to help us and give us care and guidance with any issues that arose. Once in a while, we had family meetings. One time when the boys had been moaning and groaning about having to wash and wipe the dishes, we sat down together.

"O.K.," I said. "We are going to list the family jobs on this paper. On this side, we will list your jobs and on the other half of the paper, we will have a column of the jobs for Dad and me." We started to

---

[29] Warner, Anna B. (words), Copyright © 1860, and William Bradbury (music), Copyright © 1862, "Jesus Loves Me", in the Public Domain.

write. "Jason and David – wash and dry dishes, take out the garbage, clean your own rooms, mow half the lawn each, and shovel the driveway from snow in the winter. Now Dad and Susan." I began to write and our list went longer and longer. I had to turn over the paper to finish the list. "Now, we are a family. Have we asked you to do more than your share?" They looked at the paper and the lists. They didn't complain much after that.

Overall, there were very few issues. The boys both lived with us full-time during their high school years. Those boys have been true sons to me. They have loved and respected me, and I have loved them as my own. They have both grown to be successful men with wonderful families. I love their wives, and I have 6 grandchildren!! God cared about my love of family and has blessed me beyond measure!

After Jesus, David and my family are God's greatest gifts to me, my most wonderful blessings throughout our years together.

~~~~~~~~~~~~~~~~~~~~~~~~~~~~~~~~

LET'S TALK ABOUT GOD'S CARE:

It is truly amazing how much God cares for us. When we have accepted Jesus as our Savior and Lord, we are heirs with Christ from the Father.

> When you believed, you were marked in Him with a seal, the promised Holy Spirit, Who is a deposit guaranteeing our inheritance until the redemption of those who are God's possession – to the praise of His glory.
>
> **Ephesians 1:13-14 (NIV)**

This means that God cares for us like a loving Father. He wants the best for us, even when we let Him down. He cares about what happens to us. He cares about our needs. He cares enough to sometimes discipline us in teaching us lessons that are hard to learn. He cares enough about our tough times in life to let us go through the strain to learn the most we can from trusting in Him. At other times, He showers us with gifts.

David and I led my desk rider to better behavior, giving him pride in his self-control. We also led our boys to realize that what was asked of them was little compared to the love and benefits they had at home. Even more so is God, our loving Father, caring and leading us to the best for our lives even if trials are involved along the way.

KEY TO FINDING GOD'S JOY #12:

Think of how much your Father God cares for you. Listen to Him by reading the Bible or praying. He wants the best for you. He wants to teach you. Learn through the hard lessons in life. See how He brings you through them. Learn from the everyday lessons in life. Let Him care and teach like a good parent. He is your Father and you are His heir.

PRAYERFULLY THINK ABOUT YOUR OWN LIFE WITH GOD:

It almost seems presumptuous to call ourselves the heirs of God. However, that is what He tells us in the Bible. We are His children, and He leads us like a true Shepherd. Have you ever thought of yourself as an heir of God? Can you even believe He would put you in His "will"? That is how much He cares about and loves you.

He has sent His Holy Spirit as a deposit for all we will inherit. Have you taken advantage of that deposit? If you have accepted that Jesus is Who He said He was, the Holy Spirit is within you, guiding you, praying for you, transforming you, and teaching you. What has the Holy Spirit taught you lately? How has God guided you? If the answer is you don't know, then perhaps it is time to get in contact with the Spirit within you. Ask the Holy Spirit to lead you and speak with you in your heart.

He will lead you in the way you should go. Think about your relationship with the Father as His heir and with the Holy Spirit who guides and transforms you. What can you do to become closer to them? What are they already doing in your life? Are you thankful?

_____

_____

_____

_____

_____

_____

_____

_____

_____

_____

_____

_____

_____

_____

A Song of
God's Strong Arms

He will hold me fast.
- Ada Habershon

I know this is not true for some young women, but as I grew up, I always dreamed of becoming a mother. To hold a baby, my baby, related to me through the DNA of all my ancestors was a desire I had from a very young age. I love children!

When I was married to my first husband, it became clear to me very quickly that having a baby under the circumstances of my life at that time would not be good for any child. We did not even try.

After marrying David, I was blessed with two wonderful stepsons who treated me as a mother. I remember David Jr. asking me in our first year of marriage, "Are we going to soon be having a little brother or sister?"

When I married David, I had known at the time that he had the two children and wasn't very enthusiastic about starting over since the boys were close to being teenagers. However, there was a secret place in my heart that hoped that somehow we could work it out to have a baby. I believe that if David had known the depth of my desire, we would have tried.

But there was no time. This was not to be. Toward the beginning of our marriage, I had some endocrine problems with an imbalance in my hormones, and later I developed fibroid tumors in my uterus. My gynecologist shared the bad news. "You really should have a hysterectomy, Susan. The one fibroid is as big as a grapefruit!" My endocrinologist suggested that I have a complete hysterectomy, removing my ovaries as well. She thought that would help some of my endocrine problems. This was not the news I wanted to hear. Didn't God realize that I would be a loving mother to a new baby of my own? I fell into a kind of darkness, a depression that I couldn't seem to kick. I prayed about it, but the darkness remained.

The boys noticed a stray orange tabby cat in our neighborhood who was always hanging around our house at this time. "Can we adopt the cat? Please?"

We put an ad in the paper about a lost cat. There were no responses. After taking him to the vet, Marv became a member of our family. Knowing my hysterectomy was coming close, this crazy cat, Marv, became my "baby". He would sit in my lap and snuggle, rather unusual for a cat. However, it became obvious that I was having a problem with this also. My eyes were tearing up, and I was sneezing and clogged up all of the time when near Marv. I had developed an allergy to cats.

The day came for me to have my hysterectomy. David had decided that while I was in the hospital, he was going to take Marv to a new home in a barn he had seen on a farm in the country with many cats who would welcome him. I was holding onto Marv with all my might as I escaped to the laundry room for a cry. I was grieving the child I would never have. I was grieving the loss of my new buddy, Marv. Tears were flowing as David stepped into the room.

"We have to leave now, Susan, or we're going to be late. Why don't you give me Marv and get ready to go?"

My crying became sobbing. I reluctantly handed Marv to David. I stood there with nothing in my arms. No Marv. No cuddling in the future. No baby. No little arms to hug his or her mama. It was almost unbearable. While seeing myself handing Marv to David, the Holy Spirit spoke to my soul. Marv had come to our house for a purpose. His purpose from God was to help me with this day. This sadness was something psychologically stirring in my heart that day. God did not let me stuff it down trying to be brave. I was having to physically hand over Marv, and in doing so, it let out all of my heartbreak. It was symbolic of my giving up the baby I would never know.

God's strong arms were around me through this terrible sadness in my life. A song made famous by Keith and Kristyn Getty, *He Will Hold Me Fast*, fills my heart.

> *I am precious in His sight, He will hold me fast;*
> *those He saves are His delight, He will hold me fast.*
> *He will hold me fast. He will hold me fast.*
> *For my Savior loves me so. He will hold me fast.*[30]

I thanked God for Marv that day and in days to come. God had given me a way to release my feelings of grief. There was joy in knowing that God would care about me enough to bring Marv to our home for but a short period of time. A true gift!

~~~~~~~~~~~~~~~~~~~~~~~~~~~~~~~~

---

[30] Habershon, Ada, Copyright © 1908, "He Will Hold Me Fast", in the Public Domain.

LET'S TALK ABOUT GOD'S STRONG ARMS:

Some of you may have had to face a hysterectomy which would take away all chances of having a child from your body. Some of you may have miscarried a child and feel the loss and grief that any parent would feel in that tragedy. It is difficult for someone to understand this who was able to have children. If you want children, the loss and grieving of the child that never would be or has died in the womb rips at your soul.

How can you possibly find joy in that? Remember, joy is not always happiness. Joy is that deep-down knowledge that God is with you through your heartbreak. Often it takes a long time to grieve this loss, but you can take comfort in knowing the God of the universe who loves you is holding you fast.

God is with us wherever we are in whatever state we are existing. You may not have had a hysterectomy or lost a child in the womb, but no life is free from troubles. If we have put our faith in God, He is with us. Always. He held me fast through my grief and brought me to peace in my circumstances that only God can give. Peace and acceptance. If we have given our hearts to God, He will not leave us. The worst may come. He will not leave us. Once again the Psalmist writes in the Bible:

> If I go up to the heavens, You are there;
> If I make my bed in the depths, You are there.
> If I rise on the wings of the dawn, if I settle on the far
> side of the sea, even there Your hand will guide me,
> Your right hand will hold me fast.
> **Psalm 139:8-10 (NIV)**

In talking about this loss, I do not want to diminish the extraordinary gift which God has given me in David Jr. and Jason. This was part of God's plan for me. He knew how much I wanted children and wouldn't be able to have them. He provided me with the best sons a mom could hope for in her life. God had this! He has brought joy in so many ways in my relationship with the boys and now their wives, Andrea and Mish. What gifts those young women are in my life!

I am blessed with six wonderful grandchildren whom all know me as Grandma – Kathryn, David III, Andrew, Jason Jr., Anthony, and Emma. We were there at each of their births. David and I have watched each one grow into a loving person, and we enjoyed so many activities with them over the years. We have all had visits to the zoo, the arboretum, miniature golf, go-carting, water boats squirting each other, water balloon wars, plays, movies, golf, and I-FLY where they took turns being blown high into the air and floating many feet above the ground.

Before each started 3rd grade during the entire summer, I read that child a book my dad had gotten when he was little. Dad had read it to me. *The Adventures of Pinocchio[31]*. It was not the Disney version, but a very old version written by C. Collodi and illustrated by Atillio Mussino. I had also read it at the beginning of each school year to my new class. The life lessons in that book are amazing, but the pictures are a little scary. It was a bonding time between each grandchild and me during the summer. After reading it, that child would write a marionette play and the siblings or cousins who could read would take part in putting on a marionette show for the family. Such fun!

We have also been to many of the grandchildren's sports games, dance, pom pom, or cheerleading shows. The best times have been overnights when we could play games in the backyard, catch

---

[31] Collodi, Carlo (words), Attilio Mussino (illustrations), Carol Della Chiesa (translation from Italian to English), Copyright © 1926, New York, NY: Macmillan Company.

fireflies, sit on the quilt and read books, and play table games before bed. For me, the most special moments came when putting them to bed and singing to them. I always ended with *Oh How He Loves You and Me*[32] by Kurt Kaiser, and we would put all the names of every relative into the song... Mommy, Daddy, Grandpa, Grandma, each cousin's name, aunts, uncles, great-grandma, etc. I remember having Anthony over by himself one night. When I finished singing and he was almost asleep, I heard, "That was beautiful, Grandma." Such joy in those grandkids!

I worried that if they found out I wasn't their "real" grandma, they might not love me as much. When the oldest, Kathryn, was about 6, my mom and I were playing a board game with her. Somehow we got to talking about her beautiful blond hair. "It's like yours, Grandma," she said. Then out of nowhere came, "Oh wait. That's right. We have different germs."

Mom and I giggled as she obviously had been told about genes and why she had 3 grandmas. We went right on with our game. Love had not changed. I was still Grandma.

God's strong arms have gotten me through disappointment leading to pure joy! My prayer is that each of my grandchildren and their children come to know Jesus in a personal relationship as their Savior and Lord.

KEY TO FINDING GOD'S JOY #13:

If you are facing terrible disappointments in your life, rest in Jesus. If you also faced the difficulty of not having the children for which you always hoped, rest in Jesus' strong arms. Just pray and rest. He

[32] Kaiser, Kurt, Copyright © 1975, "Oh How He Loves You and Me", Los Angeles, California: Word Music, Inc.

will hold you tightly. In those arms, you will find joy deep down in your heart in the form of peace.

PRAYERFULLY THINK ABOUT YOUR OWN LIFE WITH GOD:

Do you think your life's ambitions will never be fulfilled? Maybe it is not children but a job or education you want. Maybe it is finding the right spouse just for you. Rest in Jesus' strong arms. Is he not stronger than any problem you may have? What are you facing that is difficult? Have you talked to God about it? Have you been able to rest in His arms knowing he is there with you? Do you realize how much He loves you and understands your hurts or desires? Take a few moments to reflect on these questions. Remember, you don't have to answer every question. One may stand out to you and give you the desire to write. God bless you as you wrestle with the difficulties in your life.

_____

_____

_____

_____

_____

_____

_____

_____

_____

_____

_____

14
A Song of
God's Awesomeness and Power

Joyful, joyful, we adore Thee,
God of glory, Lord of love;
Hearts unfold like flowers before Thee,
Praising Thee, their sun above.
- Henry Van Dyke

I squeezed my eyes closed. Oh, if I could just make this day go away. My stomach lunged in my body as we pulled up to the hangar in Sonoma, California. It felt like tiny gymnasts were doing push-ups in my stomach. Wanting to appear brave, I grasped the handle of the car door, shoved it open, and stood up.

My brother-in-law, Bud, had said I was in for the ride of my lifetime. At this moment, I wasn't so sure of that! When Bud had first offered to take me up in his World War II Ryan open-cockpit airplane, I thought that the idea was great. As the time drew near, I hesitated. My husband looked as though he wasn't worried at all, and he was afraid of heights! Was I the only one who was beginning to feel scared to death? Open cockpit! Have you ever had to face something that had you worried? Maybe it sounded like a good idea when it came up, but as the event approached all you wanted to do was run?

We prepared for take-off as Bud opened the hangar door, and I stared at the smallest plane I had ever seen. The blue and yellow Ryan was just a bit bigger than a large van. As David helped to roll the plane out of the hangar, I donned the weirdest-looking headgear. The brown flaps pulled tightly over my ears and hooked under my chin. The headphones were built into the flaps, and I looked just like the World War II German Red Baron. All I needed was a scarf around my neck.

Yes Sir! Ready for take off! (I think!)

I climbed into the front seat of the plane, and Bud instructed me. "Now Susan. Do not touch the foot pedals in the front or touch your knees to the knee control. If you do, you will be taking control of the airplane." Not a good idea! Bud climbed into the rear seat, set a control, got out, and tried to push the propeller. As he did, he jumped out of the way. On the third attempt, the propeller clicked and began to spin. Bud jumped into the pilot's seat behind me, and we were on our way. We taxied to the starting point of the runway.

"Oh, God. What if I fall out of the plane? It's an open cockpit!! What if something happens to Bud while flying? What if we crash? Be with us, Lord!"

My stomach was once again doing flip-flops as the plane began to roll down the runway. Faster and faster and faster - and we were in the air! I looked at the spinning ground below me as the huge buildings below became smaller and smaller.

Gazing through the windshield, the beautiful crystal blue sky rose in front of me. I noticed that looking through the spinning propeller right in front of me was a bit like looking through a hummingbird's wings. My racing heart slowed, and excitement took over from fear. I had never been so high in the open air before, and it was exhilarating! Soaring over fields, hills, and then mountains, I hung on for dear life. Then I saw it. Rising in the distance in front of me, the clear blue Pacific Ocean appeared. I had never seen it before, and the sight left me awe-struck.

The words of the song that came to me that day were from *Joyful, Joyful, We Adore Thee.*

> *All Thy works with joy surround Thee, Earth and heav'n reflect Thy rays.*
> *Stars and angels sing around Thee, center of unbroken praise.*
> *Field and forest, vale and mountain, flowery meadow, flashing sea.*

Chanting bird and flowing fountain, call us to rejoice in Thee.[33]

After the way the day had started, thoughts occurred to me, which I wouldn't have expected. The earth was so beautiful. I felt praise to God in my heart for the plush green fields of grapes, the hills rising and falling, and the freezing air of being above the craggy mountains. The Pacific blue ocean shimmering in the sunlight extended beyond my eyesight. God's creation was singing that day.

My fear of flying turned to the awe of the Lord. That God had brought about man to invent an air machine that could soar over His creation and above the mountains like the birds was amazing in itself. Our God is an awesome and powerful God. There is joy in His creation!

~~~~~~~~~~~~~~~~~~~~~~~~~~~~~~

LET'S TALK ABOUT GOD'S AWESOMENESS AND POWER:

I am a worrier. It is a sin that I work on with God. I call it a sin, because when I worry I am not putting my trust in the God who loves me. I am thinking only of myself or others. Are you a worrier? Do you worry about your children, your husband, or other family members? Are you afraid to try new things? Do you get all set to do something exciting and then fall into fear before it ever happens? Sometimes, do your worries paralyze you, and you miss out on the happiness or awesome time you could have enjoyed?

I learned a while ago that my first name Susan means "like a lily". I thought that was kind of a wimpy name meaning. What about names

---

[33] Van Dyke, Henry (Words), Copyright © 1907, "Joyful, Joyful, We Adore Thee", in the Public Domain. Ludwig van Beethoven (Music), Copyright © 1824, "Ode to Joy", in the Public Domain.

with meanings like "bold one" or "precious in God's sight"? This was not to be. I was "like a lily".

One day I found the verses in the Bible which have become my passage:

> And which of you by worrying can add a single day to his life's span? And why are you worried about clothing? Notice how the lilies of the field grow; they do not labor nor do they spin thread for cloth, yet I say to you that not even Solomon in all his glory clothed himself like one of these. But if God so clothes the grass of the field, which is *alive* today and tomorrow is thrown into the furnace, will He not much more clothe you? You of little faith!... But seek first His kingdom and His righteousness, and all these things will be provided to you. So do not worry about tomorrow; for tomorrow will worry about itself. Each day has enough trouble of its own.
>
> **Matthew 6:27-30 and 33-34 (NASB)**

Being "like a lily" meant God would watch over and take care of me. What an awesome God to teach me that through His word. Reading God's word daily for His wisdom and praying helps to remind me that I need not worry. God has this.

Retired Lutheran Bishop Wayne Miller, a very old friend of mine from 3rd grade through Augustana College together, posted on Facebook recently. I asked him for permission to quote from his post. "WORRY is the unholy matrimony between FEAR and POWERLESSNESS. Fear, in and of itself, is good and necessary. In the face of threat, it produces a "fight or flight" response that may well save our lives. But when fear is separated from any meaningful response to remove the danger, the only thing that remains is the paralysis of WORRY. WORRY is a time machine, relentlessly propelling us either into an idealized past that never really existed and to which we can never return or into a utopian future (in a perfect world) that we cannot attain. And because of this, WORRY is a thief, stealing from us the one thing we do have in the palm of our hand; which is, NOW. I am increasingly convinced that WORRY is the engine that is driving our civilization into dysfunction and possibly toward the brink of self-annihilation... And the antidote for all this worry… the completely accessible but ever-elusive vaccine… is to embrace what is HERE, NOW - to engage with life as it is in the present with gratitude for all that is good in it, with humility and sometimes contrition for all that is broken in it, with the serenity to accept what I cannot change, the courage to change what I can, and the wisdom to know the difference.. and perhaps a little prayer asking God to bless what deserves blessing and to redeem what stands in need of redemption... Which, if we can pull it off leaves us with well, with very little to worry about."

How awesome is our God that we can place all our worries in God's hands and live in the NOW? He is our power when we fear.

God is also powerful and amazing in his creation as I realized in my open-cockpit airplane ride. If you are feeling worried, sad, or just out of touch with God, first go to His word in the Bible to read His truths. Pray. Then, go to see His creation. Find a park and enjoy the birds and the flowers and the butterflies. Hike a mountain with friends or swim in a beautiful lake or ocean. See what God has created in our world. Take a walk down a country road and find a big tree that speaks to you. It has survived there for years and years. Imagine who or what has gone by that tree in the past. Know that God created that tree and has been there seeing it survive through storms and winter blasts. Will He not do the same for you who has been created in his image? Praise God! Our God is the powerful creator of the world and of you. Find joy and God's peace in His Word and also through praising God in prayer and in His creation!

> Shout for joy to God, all the earth! Sing the glory of His name; make His praise glorious! Say to God, "How awesome are your deeds! So Great Your power...
>
> **Psalm 66:1-3 (NIV)**

KEY TO FINDING GOD'S JOY #14:

Give your worries to God every day in prayer. Write them down in the morning and then tear them up and throw them away. Don't worry needlessly. The day will take care of itself with God's guidance. Be amazed when God gets you through what was worrying you. If you are worrying and that worry becomes reality, you have had to go through your trauma twice! Give your worries to God and find joy deep down that He is with you in whatever you are worrying about that day. Sometimes be blown away by the creation of God and let it take you away from worries or fears. God has given us so many gifts in nature. Let them soothe your soul and bring you joy and peace.

PRAYERFULLY THINK ABOUT YOUR OWN LIFE WITH GOD:

If you are a worrier, have you figured out that it can hurt you in the long run? Worry can make you sick. Are you a perfectionist that worries that everything must be perfect before it can happen? When you worry, have you found a way to let it go? Do you get into God's Word every day to find God's lesson for you that day? Do you pray and give your worries to the almighty and powerful God?

Think of an example of when your fear and your powerlessness to do anything about that fear robbed you of the moment. What was that? Did you come to peace about it or do you need to try something new? Try writing down those worries each morning and throwing them away. Have you tried getting out in nature and letting God awe you with His power and beauty? It is God's power that can free you when you are powerless. What are a few thoughts you have after you have read this chapter? Do you have a plan for your worry in the future?

_____

_____

_____

_____

_____

_____

_____

_____

_____

_____

_____

_____

_____

_____

_____

_____

A Song of God's Refuge

Fear not I am with thee. O be not dismayed.
- K.

"*Oh, Lord God. Not something else wrong with my body!*" I had already had my accident, my complete hysterectomy, and the endocrine hormonal problem. Standing in front of the ER x-ray machine, I prayed that this problem could go away with a simple pill. What if I had pneumonia!?

After the x-ray, the ER doctor entered. "Well, the good news is that you don't have pneumonia. The bad news is that both of the lymph nodes on either side of your aorta are enlarged. You also seem to have some lesions on your lungs. You should see your general practitioner, but when we see this, it can be either cancer or sarcoidosis."

Sarcoidosis? What was that?

"Most likely it is sarcoidosis since both lymph nodes are enlarged. Sarcoidosis is a disease that can strike many parts of the body with lesions that are formed. It looks as though you have some on your lungs. That's why you are coughing."

118

Of course, a million scenarios were going through my head at the time. How do you get rid of sarcoidosis? Is it deadly? Unfortunately, I am certain that many of you have had those visits to a doctor where you find you have a new battle with some disease on your hands.

This was the start of another health journey for me. After visiting my general doctor, it was decided we would just watch it for a while. They were fairly certain it was sarcoidosis and not cancer, because sarcoid is genetically prevalent in those with Scandinavian or African backgrounds. I am pure Scandinavian.

Looking in the mirror one morning, a big lump lurking there underneath the upper outside corner of my left eyelid stared me in the face. What was that?!

Also, I could see the lips moving in children's mouths at school, but I wasn't hearing them clearly. I was teaching in a warehouse-type schoolroom where their little voices would go up and get lost in the ceiling. My sinuses were all plugged up right to my ears!

Now laying on the CAT scan table for the doctor to have a look at my sinuses, I wondered if you could get sarcoidosis lesions in your sinuses. When the scan was finished, the technician said, "How do you live with all that in your head?" I knew it must be bad.

The disease was only getting worse, and I still was not positive that they had the right diagnosis. My eye doctor wanted to remove the lump under my eyelid in case it was cancer. However, that would result in dry eye forever. I declined, hoping I had sarcoidosis there.

My doctor explained, "There are lesions in your sinuses, on your lungs, probably under your eyelid in your lacrimal gland, and your heart is enlarged. After about seven to nine years, the disease usually goes into remission. Sometimes it doesn't. I could put you on a beta-blocker, but there are side effects."

A new lesion finally appeared on my skin which was easy to biopsy. I had sarcoidosis.

I prayed each day that I could get through the school day. Reading a book to the children, which I always did after lunch, was difficult. I gagged from the loosening sinus clog from talking and would run to the hallway in case I would throw up. Not a pretty picture to explain, but the truth. The fatigue was terrible. These were "Why me, God?" moments. Was it hard to find joy in the midst of this? Yes. And yet, deep in my heart, I knew that God was with me. He always was there. Prayer and reading the Bible certainly helped me concentrate on God rather than on my problems. God brought scripture that I had read previously to mind in my lowest times:

> God is our refuge and strength, an ever-present help in trouble.
>
> **Psalm 46:1 (NIV)**

God was there with me! His joy was there in the form of peace that He would get me through this time. Seven years after being diagnosed, my sarcoidosis went into remission.

Without God in my life, this would have been much harder to survive with the uncertainty of how it would go. Jesus was my foundation to stand on throughout the seven years. The hymn that rings loudly in my ears is *How Firm a Foundation.*

> *How firm a foundation, ye saints of the Lord, is laid for your faith in His excellent word. What more can He say than to you He hath said? To you who for refuge to Jesus have fled. Fear not I am with thee. O be not dismayed.*

For I am thy God; I will still give thee aid. I'll strengthen thee, help thee, and cause thee to stand, upheld by My gracious omnipotent hand.[34]

Not long after feeling better, plantar fasciitis of the tendon in my right foot rose its ugly head.

"I will not have another one of those painful cortisone shots in my heel," I told the doctor. "I would rather have surgery on my foot than another shot." Amazing how that surgery seemed like nothing after the bout with sarcoidosis.

~~~~~~~~~~~~~~~~~~~~~~~~~~

LET'S TALK ABOUT GOD'S REFUGE:

Does it ever seem to you that you get more problems than most? Do your problems become overwhelming to you? Perhaps they are not health problems but of another category. Do you worry what people may be thinking behind your back? These were my thoughts: *"She must not take care of herself. If she would just lose weight, I bet that would solve many problems. She must not eat healthy food. How can something else be happening to her?"* And worst of all: *"Maybe she is a hypochondriac."*

I had to hand these thoughts over to God, also. *"Oh God. Please take these thoughts from my head. Help me to know what to do to avoid health problems and help me follow Your word and find peace. Help me to find refuge in You."*

---

[34] K. (words), Copyright © 1787, Anonymous (music), "How Firm a Foundation", Joseph Funk, Copyright © 1832, *A Compilation of Genuine Church Music,* Winchester, Virginia: J.W. Hollis (1832), in the Public Domain.

Billy Graham said, "'Good' people do not escape suffering in this life. The Bible lists in Hebrews 11 the heroes of the faith, both Jew and Gentile, who were tortured, imprisoned, stoned, torn apart, and killed by the sword... In America today, being a Christian is sometimes equated with having good health. Some popular nutrition and psychology publications recommend that a sound body may require a strong spiritual life. Many of these writers lean toward a hybrid of Eastern religious thought and humanistic psychology, but others have been biblically sound. I believe that exercise and proper eating habits are very important, since the Bible says that the body is God's holy temple, but I don't think that superbodies equate with committed Christian discipleship. Some of the greatest saints I've known have been those with physical infirmities."[35]

I think what Billy Graham said about some of the greatest saints having physical infirmities shows that when you go through these tough times in life, you have to cling to the Lord to survive it. In doing so, you learn to and need to depend on the Lord. No one can easily get through physical infirmities with joy in their heart without a strong dependence on God.

Jesus healed people in His time on earth. He instantly healed a dying woman who just reached out to touch His cloak! The Bible says:

Jesus Christ is the same yesterday, today and forever.
Hebrews 13:8 (NIV)

He still has that same power through the Holy Spirit to heal us and restore us in our times of deepest need. Does it always happen that we are healed from our physical diseases? No. Does it always happen that we are freed from our biggest problems? No. Do you

---

[35] Graham, Billy, Copyright © 1991, *Hope for the Troubled Heart: Finding God in the Midst of Pain,* Nashville, Tennessee: W Publishing Group, p. 37. All rights reserved. Used by permission..

remember our conversation about how God works for good for those who love Him? In this world, we don't always see the good that comes from God. It may come after our time here. Also, sometimes, God can teach us more about Him through our problems than by taking them away. Give your burdens to God and see what He will do.

KEY TO FINDING GOD'S JOY #15:

Believe that God is there. He is your refuge and strength. No matter what problem you have with health or otherwise, God has promised to be our refuge. He will be your safe place, a place where you can sometimes hide from the horrible things of life. Find peace in that. Wrap yourself in the Lord. Find your joy knowing God is truly blanketing you with His peace in whatever you may be going through at this time. Imagine this blanket of peace and refuge covering you with God's peace and joy. You will eventually be able to stand again and look at the world with joy in your heart.

PRAYERFULLY THINK ABOUT YOUR OWN LIFE WITH GOD:

God is our safe place. Whether He miraculously heals us or helps us through every day of our issues, He wants to be your place to hide and rest in Him. Do you have an illness or another catastrophe that has completely interfered with your life? What is it? Are you depending on God? Has this made you angry or doubting in God? Have you run to God for refuge in your most difficult times? That's what He wants you to do. Think about these times in your life. If you do not have a difficult time right now, what could you do differently next time a trial comes? Take a few minutes to reflect.

16

A Song of God's Gifts

Praise to the Lord the Almighty
The King of creation!
- Joachim Neander, Catherine Winkworth
and Stralsund Gesangbuch

Eight full years went by without many difficulties. Praise God! They were exciting years. David and I traveled, enjoying every moment of life. We spent our 25th wedding anniversary in Hawaii. God had sheltered me under His wings as my refuge and strength. Now He was pouring out his blessings in gifts I couldn't imagine. We are thankful in the hard times and especially thankful in the great times.

When I think of these days, I can only praise the Lord in song.

Praise to the Lord who over all things so wondrously reigneth. Shelters thee under His wings; yea so gently sustaineth. Hast thou not seen how thy desires ever have been granted in what He ordaineth. Praise to the Lord, O let all that is in me adore Him. All that hath life and breath come now with praises before Him. Let the amen sound from His people again. Gladly for all we adore Him.[36]

The year before my dad died, Mom and Dad moved to a condo and cleaned out their attic at the old house. Mom found a very fat envelope which she handed to me.

"You should have these, if you want them."

"What are they?" I asked.

"Your Grandma Berg saved all the letters that Dad wrote home during World War II. He wrote to different members of the family, and Grandma kept them all in one place. I think there are hundreds of letters in here."

Curious, I opened the envelope while sitting on my sick dad's bed. I pulled out one of the letters that turned out to be the best letter in the whole envelope. I didn't know it then, but I think God allowed me to find it and have that special time with my dad. I read the letter out loud to dad. It had been written to his little sister, Ellie, who was twelve when he left for war. In it, he told of his ship coming upon 70 men on a floater net in the Pacific Ocean from the destroyer, the U.S.S. Bush. The ship had been sunk by 3 kamikazes. Dad had written the letter after the censorship of letters had been lifted, so he was able to give some details. He and another guy had helped a sailor who was just about dead and had given him artificial respiration. Dad was praying that he was doing it right, and he was thrilled when the man came out of it and lived. They were able to

---

[36] Neander, Joachim (words), Copyright © 1680, Catherine Winkworth (translator), 1863, "Praise to the Lord the Almighty", in the Public Domain, Stralsund Gesangbuch (Music), Copyright © 1665, "Lob Den Herren", in the Public Domain.

put him on a hospital ship headed for the states. I was able to look at my dad and say, "Dad! You were a hero!"

My dad had never talked about the war to me. He mumbled something about just doing his job, but I am thankful that I was able to tell him that he was a hero before he died. God led me to that particular letter. A true gift!

My dad passed away in 1996, the year after I read him his letter. I grieved that loss for a long time. I still miss him. I remember so clearly as Dad was dying that I always wanted to listen to Anton Dvorak's *2nd Movement in his New World Symphony.* It gave me such peace, but I didn't know why. One day I told Barb that I was listening to it over and over again. (Dad probably would have liked to hear a bit of Bobby Vinton or another hymn once in a while). However, I would listen at least once or twice every day.

Barb said, "Susan, don't you know what the words are to that music?"

"No, I don't. The music just gives me peace."

"The words are *Going home, going home. I'm just going home. Quiet-like, slip away. I'll be going home. It's not far, just close by; Jesus is the Door. Work all done, laid aside; Fear and grief no more.*[37] No wonder you are listening to that over and over. You feel God's peace."

I had been listening to the music and had no idea of the powerful words which went with the symphony. Even so, God had given me peace. I looked up the rest of the words. The lyrics end with:

---

[37] Fisher, William Arms (words), Copyright © 1922, "Going Home", in the Public Domain, Anton Dvorak (music), Copyright © 1893, " 2nd Movement 'Largo', Symphony No. 9 in E Minor Op. 95 (From the New World)", in the Public Domain.

Every tear wiped away, pain and sickness gone. Wide awake there with Him, peace goes on and on. Going home, going home, I'll be going home. See the light. See the sun. I'm just going home.[38]

That song helped me through that time as I thought of God welcoming Dad with open arms and Dad's pain all gone. Praise God! Another gift from God! Dad is buried at the Great Lakes Military Cemetery in Holly, Michigan. Since I am far away from his burial place, I often look at pictures on the website for this cemetery. One day this beautiful picture of the military stones and a cross in the sky formed by rising sun and clouds came onto the site. It gives me peace every time I look at it.

Dad's burial place: Great Lakes Military Cemetery in Holly, Michigan - Picture taken by Mike Mishler from Lincat Photography

---

[38] Fisher, William Arms (words), Copyright © 1922, "Going Home", in the Public Domain, Anton Dvorak (music), Copyright © 1893, " 2nd Movement 'Largo', Symphony No. 9 in E Minor Op. 95 (From the New World)", in the Public Domain.

I didn't read the rest of my dad's letters until about two years after Dad passed away. It was too hard. When I did start to read them, I read all day, all night, and all the next day to get through them. I couldn't believe how Dad's words just flowed on the pages. The dad I knew was a very quiet man of few words, but here, in these letters, I heard his voice. The voice changed depending on to whom he was writing.

Dad was only seventeen when he joined the navy. To his dad, he talked about the business of war and what he would do for a job when he got out of the navy. To his twin brother and sister who were 15 when he left, he gave advice and told them he wished he only had to worry about school and teachers now. To his mom, he talked about his feelings, about his communications from church, and about the prayers he appreciated. To his little sister, he bragged a bit. Mainly, I could see how Dad clung to his faith in Jesus as he endured the pressures and horrors of war.

I researched the U.S.S. Bush and found a website where sailors who were rescued or sailors who were part of the rescuing could write in their memories. I sent in dad's letter, the one I had pulled out randomly from the letters in the envelope. The webmaster wrote back. His dad had been one of those rescued. He wanted me to thank my dad if he was still alive.

A few days later, I received an email from a man, Dave, whose dad was given artificial respiration that day on dad's ship. He had talked with many sailors from dad's ship, the U.S.S. Pakana, who had given artificial respiration, but all their guys that they tried to rescuscitate hadn't made it. Here was dad's letter saying that his guy had lived. Dave told me he thought it was probably my dad who saved his dad. Then he went on to tell me all the people and things in his life that wouldn't be there if Dad had not saved his dad's life. Needless to say, I cried throughout his list. Mom, David, and I attended a U.S.S. Bush reunion in Pittsburgh where we met Dave and his dad. It was a moment I will never forget.

I published a book using my dad's letters from World War II through an educational publisher of history for kids to young adults. It was *Voyage to Victory: The Voice of a Sailor in the Pacific 1943-1945.* I also became a WWII collector of all things Dad mentioned in his letters. In his 1st letter home, he was reading a comic book on his way to boot camp. I thought it would be fun to find a Jan.1943 comic book. I found the best, *Superman.* In the issue, he was helping the U.S. Navy in the Pacific where my Dad served. That first item started my collection of hundreds of artifacts from WWII.

After I retired from teaching, I began giving World War II and the Homefront presentations to schools, churches, veterans' groups, libraries, and senior living facilities. I was also able to give presentations to each of our grandchildren's classes at some year of their education. A wonderful blessing and respite! It was easy to find joy in the good after having so many times of trouble in the past.

Emma and I posed for a picture after I presented "World War II and the Homefront" for her 5th Grade Class.

LET'S TALK ABOUT GOD'S GIFTS:

I pray that many of you have had more good days of God's gifts than of learning through the tough stuff of life. Although, there is danger in having many days of gifts, too. Just something for you to think about. You may be asking, *"Susan, you're not going to tell me now that having good days and God's gifts are a bad thing, are you?"* No. They can be a very wonderful part of your life. However, I do have a warning for you to just think about. It is not my thought, but came to me in the devotional book by Paul David Tripp:

"What we celebrate as a blessing from God can become an idol that rules and directs our hearts. It happens too easily and so subtly... The house that I once viewed as an undeserved gift from God becomes an idol that gobbles up the thoughts and desires of my heart... The theological knowledge that is the gift of the illumining ministry of the Holy Spirit becomes the reason why I look down on those who don't know what I know... It's the good things that replace the Giver of those things in my heart... We all have wandering hearts. We are still tempted to put the gift in the place that the Giver alone should occupy."[39]

I don't want to be a "downer" here. I am simply pointing out the possibility that when all is going well, we pat ourselves on the back a bit too much and forget the One from Whom all blessings flow. If I am honest with you (which I am trying to be throughout this book), when I published my first book with Dad's letters, it was a long process. I did not thank God enough for what He obviously brought to me. After all, God was the one who helped me pick out the first letter from the hundreds in which I could tell Dad that he was a hero. He was the one who brought it to my mind to share the letters with

---

[39] Taken from *New Morning Mercies: A Daily Gospel Devotional* by Paul David Tripp, Copyright © 2014, p. November 19. Used by permission of Crossway, a publishing ministry of Good News Publishers, Wheaton, IL 60187, www.crossway.org.

our 5th grade teachers, who in turn encouraged me to publish them. He was the one who helped me find the publisher.

God was helping me all along the way in the writing which has made some people find a book about war to be a "sweet" book filled with life lessons. War is never sweet. The sweetness came from the writing and relationships that my dad had with his family and buddies at sea and with the Lord. I think perhaps I was prideful. Now you can be proud of an accomplishment as long as it doesn't let you forget the Giver of all blessings. I pray in this book that you feel no "pride" from me. God is my Lord and has given me these life lessons to share with you. Praise to the Lord, the Almighty, the Giver of all good things. Let the focus be on our Lord.

KEY TO FINDING GOD'S JOY #16:

Enjoy and be thankful for every good thing the Lord brings into your life. Find joy in the Lord when you think about those things. Do not let the good thing replace the Giver of the good thing. Praise Him! Be thankful!

PRAYERFULLY THINK ABOUT YOUR OWN LIFE WITH GOD:

Well, I must say that this chapter took a different direction led by the Lord than I expected. I wanted it to be a light happy little chapter of God's good gifts, and I learned something about myself in the process. God does that, you know? Have you found yourself in a position where everything is going so well that you forget about God in your life almost completely? Don't you think that is what has happened to those who go to parks every Sunday morning or find other good things interfering with their worship of God who is the Giver of all good things?

I am not saying that you cannot worship God out of church. You certainly can every day. I question whether those not going to church are truly worshipping and thanking God in their lives. It is in their heart and soul as to what they are doing. If it has happened to you that the gift becomes an idol, what can you do about that? God wants you to enjoy your life and have fun! He wants you to be filled with joy. He simply still wants to be your God. Is he not worthy of that? Will you remember to thank Him in all things? Think on these ideas. Are you putting anything ahead of God? What can you do about that? Let's all be thankful to the Holy One for all He has done for us. Answer any of these questions or make a list of all you are thankful for today.

_____

_____

_____

_____

_____

_____

_____

_____

_____

_____

_____

_____

_____

A Song of God's Hope

In every high and stormy gale
My anchor holds within the veil.
- Edward Mote

*W*alking in the mornings was a special treat, until it wasn't. Pain seemed to be settling into the places where my muscles or tendons attached to the bones. At times, nerve pain was going up and down my body. I also had a little tickle cough that was continuous. I saw many doctors, but it wouldn't go away. In the summer of 2011, Mom and I went on a cruise to Nova Scotia from Boston. We had a great time, and I felt pretty good during our trip except while sitting for long times at a show. After we returned from the trip, the next morning things changed.

"What is going on here?" I said. "My right arm won't raise at all!" I raced into the bathroom to look at my face. Did I have a stroke? I smiled and stuck out my tongue. All seemed well on the stroke front. What was wrong now?

I called my doctor who said it was probably a rotator cuff and to see my orthopedic surgeon. The surgeon took a scan of my shoulder and neck. The results shocked me. "There is no way for me to help you. You need to see a neurosurgeon."

I went to my neurosurgeon, Dr. Johnson, who looked at the MRI he ordered. "Susan, you have bone in your neck where there shouldn't be any bone."

"Is it arthritis?" I asked.

"No. It isn't. If I hadn't seen you walk in today, looking at this, I would think you were a quadriplegic. Your spinal cord is completely cut off from the spinal fluid trying to get through it. You are going to need a neck specialist."

"But I want you!" I trusted this man. He was the head surgeon for the US Marines. He was kind. I didn't want to go to a new doctor.

"I can't do this kind of surgery. It is way too extensive." He recommended 3 doctors, but his assistant said, "Take Dr. Nockels."

In the meantime, while waiting to get into Dr. Nockels, Dr. Johnson ordered an Electromyographic Nerve Test (EMG). I told my physical therapist, Joe, that I was going to get the test that afternoon. He asked, "Is David going with you?"

"No," I said. "I think I will be fine."

"I think David should go with you, Susan." What was this test that David should go with me? Joe didn't tell me anymore.

Poor David did go with me. We entered the testing room, and the first thing the doctor doing the test said was, "Dr. Johnson wants me to do all four limbs and your back?!!!" There was incredible horror on his face.

I knew I was in for something unpleasant. The EMG involves needles and electric shock on nerves in the body. Usually, only one limb is done. It tests for damaged nerves, and since Dr. Johnson thought I should have been a quadriplegic, he wanted to know the damage done all over my body. Yes! This test was very painful, and I made many awful noises as it proceeded. However, my poor husband had to sit there and watch me go through the pain. It is always harder to see someone you love go through pain than it is to go through it yourself. Somehow when you yourself are going through it, you can summon the courage and the knowledge that it will soon be over. David could only see the pain. I was glad, however, that David was there to drive my limp body home that afternoon.

Our appointment was expedited because of the seriousness of my case. God was taking care of me again. Dr. Nockels knew immediately what I had. Ossification of the Posterior Longitudinal Ligament (OPLL). This is a genetic Asian disease where the ligament inside of your vertebrae next to your spinal cord begins to turn to bone when you are born. Then the bone continues to grow toward the spinal cord. As you get older, it may grow slowly and you never know you have the problem. However, if you are like me, the bone grows at a faster rate and cuts off your spinal cord, squashing it.

"I can't have an Asian genetic disease," I said. "I'm 100% Norwegian."

"Well, even if it was thousands of years ago, an Asian was in your DNA family tree somewhere."

God granted me a miracle in all of this fearful mess. Dr. Nockels did his residency in San Francisco where there were many Asians. He saw OPLL a lot, and he was not happy with the way the complex surgery to help this condition was being done in the USA. He left and went to Japan for two years to study how to do my surgery. It involved going in from the back of the neck and moving the spinal cord away from the boney ligament. Then a cage had to be built around the procedure to keep everything in place. He was probably the only doctor in the US who had done such a study, and God brought me to him. I had hope that my arm would no longer be paralyzed from the shoulder to the elbow and that other nerve pains would disappear.

I had the surgery, and it was 1½ years before I could raise both arms completely. These days of recuperation were amazing. My husband, David, was my faithful nurse. David sacrificed for me. He was up every 4 hours during the night to give me medicine after surgery. He took care of everything around the home. What a blessing that man is in my life!

I had an email group of 114 relatives and friends who were praying for me every day. Monthly, I would update them on how I was doing and if I was making progress. They sent cards of encouragement or brought food to the house.

And God. Oh, my Lord God! He gave me that peace every day that truly passes all understanding. I never seemed to worry during this time, and as you know from the last few chapters, worry is usually something I have to constantly give to God. I often sang songs like *The Solid Rock*.

> *On Christ the solid rock I stand; All other ground is*
> *sinking sand.*
> *All other ground is sinking sand.*[40]

Another was

> *It Is Well With My Soul.*

---

[40] Mote, Edward (Words), Copyright © 1834, William Batchelder Bradbury (Music), Copyright © 1863, "The Solid Rock", in the Public Domain.

*When peace like a river attendeth my way, When
sorrows
like sea billows roll; Whatever my lot, Thou hast taught
me to say,
It is well, It is well with my soul.*[41]

God had given me hope that I would at some time recover from this debilitating disease.

I will never forget a particular day. I had been in therapy for a year and a half. Off to physical therapy I went. Joe was standing across the room. I raised my right arm completely to wave at him. I pointed to God as I did so. What a day!! My OPPL surgery and the inflammation afterward in both arms were healing. I could resume some regular tasks. What a blessing!

Since then, I have been diagnosed with psoriatic arthritis, which through a great rheumatologist and medicine, I am beginning to feel some relief.

In the summer of 2017, it was my turn to help my husband have hope for the future in God.

"It looks like I'm going to need a stent placed in an artery of my heart. We are scheduled for the end of the week."

My heart fell and the old nasty worry set in. What would I ever do without this man? I'm sure there are many of you who have faced a diagnosis you didn't want to hear about a loved one. It was

---

[41] Spafford, Horatio G. (Words), Copyright © 1873, "It Is Well With My Soul", in the Public Domain, Philip P. Bliss (Music and Setting 'It Is Well' or 'Ville Du Havre'), Copyright © 1876 in the Public Domain.

definitely time to pray. We spent time in prayer that night and the rest of the week.

On the day of his surgery, his cardiologist tried to place a stent in his heart, but he couldn't make the turn to the blood vessel. Open-heart surgery was scheduled for the next day. I cried as his doctor hugged me. God bless Dr. Shah!

David and I had prayed before the first surgery, but they left him under his anesthesia until the next surgery began. "If you bring him out, he will not be able to lay on his bad back, and the tubing going into his body may be disturbed," I told the doctor. I prayed alone that night, but I was not alone. God was with me throughout this terrible ordeal. God gave me hope that David would come through the surgery without a problem.

Jason and David Jr. were there with me during the open-heart surgery for their dad. Two of my friends, LaVerne and Linda, joined us and kept our minds busy with conversation and off the surgery. Jason, who hadn't met LaVerne before, kept calling her Shirley. Those old TV shows of "LaVerne and Shirley" had been on his mind to try to remember her name. We all got the giggles over it. Those two friends truly answered the call of God that day to help us keep our worries at a minimum and to hope in God.

This was another time that what seemed like a terrible surgery turned out to be a blessing. When the doctor went in to David's heart, they found three blockages and were able to bypass all three in one surgery. Thankfully, the stent for one blockage the day before had not worked. Also, before the heart surgery, David had been diagnosed with pulmonary fibrosis. When the surgeon was in his chest cavity, he pressed on David's lungs to see the extent of the pulmonary fibrosis. He said they were still pretty soft and in pretty good shape. Another blessing.

David recovered well in the following months. I tried to sacrifice for him as he had always done for me throughout my health issues, but it was hard for him to accept help. He, after all, was to be strong for me, in his mind. He did learn to accept help, however. We even had bonus help during this time. Meals were brought to our home by church friends. Men and women from the church came over for days and days to help me pull the weeds David usually kept up with when he was well. They were so giving of their time and their talents in gardening. We felt God's love flowing from them during a lousy hard job. I know it was hard. I couldn't let them be out there alone pulling our weeds. Praise the Lord for the blessing of great friends and even those who don't know you as well but are doing the work to God's glory!

This past year, I became short of breath. I mentioned it to my rheumatologist, because I had just restarted a medicine I had been off for a while. I had been short of breath when I first started it the year before this episode. She took me off the medicine, but the breathing and my heart rate only got worse. I sounded like a freight train as I simply walked across the length of our home.

Going into church for Bible study one Monday morning, I stopped mid-parking lot. Was my whole body going to give way? It was unusual to have anyone at the door when I went into the church, but God had placed three men there to work on the door.

John rushed over. "Are you O.K.?"

"I don't think so. I'm so weak."

"I'll drive you home, and Alan can follow with your car."

140

David had a doctor's appointment that morning that I didn't want him to miss, so I had thought about how we could organize things. This was during the time of the Covid 19 pandemic in 2021. I had just had my second vaccine shot 2 weeks prior to sounding like a freight train. "David, you're going to go to your doctor, because we don't even know if they will let you in the ER room because of the pandemic. I'll take an ambulance, because there is no way I can drive or sit in the waiting room."

The ambulance arrived. "Pray for me, David." My blood pressure was extremely low. I prayed all the way to the hospital. I had multiple blood clots in both lungs, more than you could count. There had to be well over 50. My heart was enlarged and damaged by the clots. I didn't realize the severity until I heard my hematologist say, "Look at all these clots on the layers of the scan! You are lucky to be alive!" We do not know yet the cause of the clots.

God had provided the men at the church door, a quick ambulance, good doctors, and peace. I felt at peace. Joy was still in my heart. I thanked God that I still had a chance at life here on earth and hope in Jesus for the future.

LET'S TALK ABOUT GOD'S HOPE:

Have you been going through challenge after challenge in your life? Living in this fallen sinful world of chaos or disease is not easy. With the new blood clots, I wondered "why" again. "Why did I have another physical problem?" But the Holy Spirit brought an idea to my attention. I realized that I was expecting special treatment, because I was a follower of the Lord. God did not bring this upon me, and how could I think the Lord would not be with me through this time also? If you know Jesus in your heart, He will never leave you in any circumstance. Even if the worst happens and you die, Jesus is with you to present you to His Father - clean in spirit and ready for Heaven's blessings. His blood was shed on the cross to pay for your sins. But God's gift of His son was not just so that Jesus could be your Savior. It was so that he could be your Lord here on earth. You are a part of His kingdom.

In Paul's letter to the Romans, he lays out what the life of one who follows God should be:

> Love must be sincere. Hate what is evil; cling to what is good. Be devoted to one another in love.
> Honor one another above yourselves. Never be lacking in zeal, but keep your spiritual fervor, serving the Lord.
> Be joyful in hope, patient in affliction, faithful in prayer.
> Share with the Lord's people who are in need.
> Practice hospitality.
>
> **Romans 12:9-13 (NIV)**

Notice God's people should be joyful because of hope and patient with those things going wrong in their lives. My Mom used to say in the pain of her final years, "It could be worse, Susan. It could be so much worse." I thank God for all the lessons I learned from my mom over the years that she lived on this earth.

God wants all of us as his people to help those in need. Throughout all of David's or my illnesses, I have been blessed with those called by God to help me and encourage me. My family and friends prayed for me every day. They prayed for my patience as I recovered, and God gave me patience. They visited me and encouraged me, and I was encouraged. These friends and family sent me cards and jokes and gifts. Many even helped pull weeds and grasses out of our ivy.

I, too, want to be a blessing to someone else who is dealing with tough times in their lives.

During my OPLL, I knew God was with me, and I learned so much about the peace and joy of God during my time of trial while leaning into Him. I really wouldn't trade one of those healing moments in the 1½ years for anything in this world. I learned, and there was peace and therefore joy in my soul. In these Bible verses, justified has to do with making our path straight through faith:

> Therefore, since we have been justified through faith, we have peace with God through our Lord Jesus Christ, through Whom we have gained access by faith into this grace in which we now stand. And we boast in the hope of the glory of God. Not only so, but we also glory in our sufferings, because we know that suffering produces perseverance; perseverance, character; and character, hope. And hope does not put us to shame, because God's love has been poured out into our hearts through the Holy Spirit, Who has been given to us.
>
> **Romans 5:1-5 (NIV)**

How wonderful are those promises?!!

KEY TO FINDING GOD'S JOY #17:

Find the peace and joy of God by letting go and letting God. I know this key sounds like "easier said than done". Sometimes we want to be so in control of everything, and that is impossible. When the craziness of disease or job troubles or relationship problems are swirling around you, God is there. Lean into Him.

PRAYERFULLY THINK ABOUT YOUR OWN LIFE WITH GOD:

Can you hear His voice? God's still small voice is saying, *"You are mine and I love you. I'll never let you go!"* There is joy in knowing that God is with us, even in our most traumatic times. Are you part of a church family who will love you and help with your care in difficult times? God wants His people to help you. Accept it from them.

In God, you can find refuge from your storm and hope for the future. Have you given Him this chance to help you? In the past or present, what has just about knocked you off your feet? What can't you control? Have you lost a job or a relationship? Will you let God help you? Will you pray and read God's word? Will you go to a Christian counselor or your doctor if you need to go? Write down some of your thoughts. God wants to know your frustrations, your troubles, and your feelings. God is in control. He is your refuge and hope for today and tomorrow.

_____

_____

_____

_____

_____

_____

_____

_____

_____

_____

A Song of God's Protection

Angels watching over me, my Lord.
- African-American Spiritual

"It's snowing so hard! I can't see the road!" David said as we traveled from Mom's home in Michigan. It was 3:00 a.m. on Christmas morning!

"What can I do to help?" I asked. "This is a blizzard!"

"Pray."

"Can you see the side of the road?" I asked. "I'm afraid we'll go off the road!"

"I can't see it. Can you see it?"

I couldn't see anything. The white of the snow was like the thickness of a white shower curtain, completely blocking our vision. "Why don't I roll down the window and put my head out? Maybe I'll be able to see the side of the road." I opened my window and put the upper half of my body through the opening. I was shaking with cold and completely wet by the time I gave up. I was beginning to panic a bit. I couldn't see the side of the road.

We had left early for the six-hour drive to arrive in time to have Christmas morning at our house in Illinois with David's family. This was hopeless. We would have to stop, but where was the side of the road so that we could pull over to park?

"Wait a minute! Are those taillights ahead of us?" asked David.

"Yes, I think they are and we're getting closer to them. They seem to be slowing down."

David just shook his head. "No one can see in this blizzard. They'll be stopping too."

We came right behind the taillights, but the car did not stop. Getting close, we could see it was not a special type of car with special lights to see in a blizzard. They would have a curtain in front of them too. But, amazingly, the car in front of us just kept going slowly, never swerving or straying from a straight line. As our overnight beautiful Christmas music played on the radio, we kept our eyes trained on those two small round red taillights.

A peace began to settle over us. We were at least with someone else in the same situation, but it was so confusing.

"How is that guy seeing the side of the road?! You can't see anything in front of you. How can he stay so steadily on the road?" I asked. I was stunned that anyone could see the road at all, but I was thankful to God for those two little red lights beckoning the way.

After an hour and a half of slowly following the lights, the snow began to let up. We were coming down to our intersection of Interstate 94, and we could actually see the signs showing us the exit was coming up ahead. The two red lights also exited at 94 going west as we followed. Now the snow had almost stopped. We had made it through the worst. At the first exit after we merged onto 94, the car we had followed put on the turn signal and started to leave the road. As we went on our way past those precious taillights, the car blinked the front lights at us. That driver knew he had saved our lives.

"I think we just followed an angel down that stretch of road," I said as "Angels We Have Heard on High" came on the radio. God had sent His protection to us through a pair of red round taillights in a blizzard. We will never know for sure, but I think God sent His angel to help us find our way. The African-American spiritual, *Angels Watching Over Me*, comes to me as I write this.

> *All night, all day. Angels watching over me, My Lord.*
> *All night, all day. Angels watching over me.* [42]

What a very special Christmas morning!

~~~~~~~~~~~~~~~~~~~~~~~~~~~~~~~~~~~~~

LET'S TALK ABOUT GOD'S PROTECTION:

Angels. As the supernatural has become of more interest in our culture in the form of the occult or even demons represented in movies, games, etc., people have also gained interest in angels. Some feel that their loved ones become angels in heaven, but this is not shown in the Bible. Angels are God's servants and messengers and protectors when sent by God to humans. Humans who know God are heirs with Jesus, children of God the Father. Some want to pray to angels, but they are not the ones to whom we should pray.

---

[42] African-American Spiritual, unknown author possibly Otis L. McCoy, "All Night, All Day", in the Public Domain.

God is the One Who answers prayers by sometimes sending His angels to those who need help. In the Bible:

> Are not all angels ministering spirits sent to serve those who will inherit salvation?
>
> **Hebrews 1:14 (NIV)**

Angels are not to be confused with the Holy Spirit which is in us, transforming, guiding, and teaching us at all times. Jesus is not to be confused with angels. Jesus is on the throne with the Father and the angels are His servants.

In Billy Graham's book, *Angels: God's Secret Agents,* Reverend Graham describes the experience of Reverend John G. Paton as a missionary in the New Hebrides Islands. One night, John and his wife had spent a night of terror as natives surrounded their mission home determined to burn down the building. In the morning, they were amazed to see all of the invaders had left. They gave God thanks. The next year, the chief of the tribe had accepted the Lord as his Savior. John asked him why his men had walked away on the night they intended to burn the mission. Billy writes, "The chief replied in surprise, 'Who were all those men you had with you there?' The missionary answered, 'There were no men there; just my wife and I.'

The chief argued that they had seen many men standing guard – hundreds of big men in shining garments with drawn swords in their hands. They seemed to circle the mission station so the natives were afraid to attack. Only then did Mr. Paton realize that God had sent His angels to protect them. The chief agreed that there was no other explanation. Could it be that God has sent a legion of angels to protect His servants whose lives were being endangered?"[43] How amazing is our God?

It is true that not all those who love the Lord experience the powerful type of experience that John Paton and his wife encountered with God's angels. But God assured us that angels would guard us and protect us through David's Psalm:

> Whoever dwells in the shelter of the Most High will rest in the shadow of the Almighty...
> For He will command his angels concerning you to guard you in all your ways; they will lift you up in their hands, so that you will not strike your foot against a stone...
> "Because he loves Me," says the Lord, "I will rescue him; I will protect him, for he acknowledges My name.
> **Psalm 91:1,11-12,14 (NIV)**

For weeks before I had my big OPLL neck surgery which was a highly dangerous procedure, I played Christian music at night and deliberately meditated on the surgery. I put myself in a beautiful place at peace, our favorite Sanibel, FL beach. In my mind, I would see the beauty. I would imagine a type of TV screen open in front of my eyes, and I could envision the surgical room where the very competent doctors and nurses were scurrying around making things just right and very clean for my surgery. I would imagine myself rolled into the operating room and there above me, I would know there was a host of angels surrounding each doctor, nurse, and me. I would thank God that He would be with me through my coming surgery, and then I would peacefully fall asleep. On the day of the surgery, I prayed, was wheeled into the operating room, and once

---

[43] Graham, Billy, Copyright © 1975, 1986, 1994, 1995, *Angels: God's Secret Agents, Dallas, Texas: Word Publishing, Pages 5-6.* All rights reserved. Used by permission.

again, I was at peace knowing that God's angels were surrounding and working with the doctors and nurses and were there with me. Protection and peace.

It is sometimes difficult in this finite world to imagine invisible beings or even those who take on human form as being there with us in our tough times. However, in our culture today, it almost seems easier for people to think about supernatural beings such as Satan, demons, or even about horoscopes, Ouija boards, tarot cards, mediums, or magic than it is to believe that there was an historic man who was God incarnate. This man loved us so much that He was willing to die on a cross for our sins to restore us into glory with God.

I am sorry to admit this, but I allowed myself to dabble in the occult culture one time after I became a Christian. It was during my uncertain times about whether or not David was capable of falling in love with me. A teacher friend of mine had gone to a woman who told about the future using your hand and tarot cards. This teacher friend was so excited about what she had learned. Unfortunately, I did not turn to God at this time, but I went to see this woman. Remember? We all still sin. Her house was filthy. I asked to use the bathroom, and the tub was filled with junk. What was I doing in a place like this? What she told me was that David was going to leave for another state.

I said, "That is impossible. He would never leave his boys."

She also told me I would never have children. Did it do me any good to know about these things ahead of time? No. It just scared me. Where did she get this knowledge? I don't believe she prayed to God to get this knowledge. How did she know this would all happen? There are supernatural beings in the world who were in control of her. It was not God. When Jane, my Behavior Disorders aide from school learned that I had done this, she couldn't believe it. She told me what God wanted me to know. He was in control of my life. I needed to depend on Him in all circumstances. I repented and never went back to her, although the pull to go was mighty. God protected me in that circumstance.

In *Angels: God's Secret Agents*, Billy Graham also makes clear that when someone accepts Jesus as their Savior, all of heaven rejoices. In Acts in the Bible, as Paul was in prison, the Philippian jailor asked him what he needed to do to be saved. Billy wrote, "Paul gave him a very simple answer. 'Believe in the Lord Jesus Christ, and thou shalt be saved.' (Acts 16:30-31) This is so simple that millions stumble over it. The one and only way you can be converted is to believe on the Lord Jesus Christ as your own personal Lord and Savior. You don't have to straighten out your life first. You don't have to try to give up some habit that is keeping you from God. You have tried all that and failed many times. You can come 'just as you are'. The blind man came just as he was. The leper came just as he was. The thief on the cross came just as he was. You can come to Christ right now wherever you are and just as you are – and the angels of heaven will rejoice!"[44]

I now think back to Barry Angel and the moment that Barb and I gave all to Jesus Christ in our hearts. The angels rejoiced!! How wonderful is that?!

KEY TO FINDING GOD'S JOY #18:

Find peace in knowing that God has provided His angels to watch over you and to help and protect you in times of trouble. Call on

---

[44] Graham, Billy, Copyright © 1975, 1986, 1994, 1995, *Angels:God's Secret Agents,* Dallas, Texas: Word Publishing, Page 213. All rights reserved. Used by permission.

the name of Jesus, and his servants will be there for you. Realize the joy when God has provided a way and or peace for you in a difficult situation.

PRAYERFULLY THINK ABOUT YOUR OWN LIFE WITH GOD:

You may never see God's angels around you until one carries you safely to Heaven. However, the Bible says they are around us through the direction of our Father God who loves us. Have you ever thought an angel has touched your life in some way? What happened? Had you called out to God for help? Have you ever dabbled in the other invisible beings besides God and his angels? Where did it get you? Did it scare you? Did it pull you away from putting your faith in the Lord Jesus?

Try to imagine God's angels surrounding you each night before you go to sleep and thank God for His protection and love. God wants you to be at peace. Joy comes in that peace. Take a moment to admit if you have been tempted by other supernatural beings in this world. Then, reflect on angels in your life and how God has protected you at times.

_____

_____

_____

_____

_____

_____

_____

A Song of
God's Peace

What a treasure I have in this wonderful peace
Buried deep in the heart of my soul....
I am resting tonight in this wonderful peace
Resting sweetly in Jesus' control....
- Warren D. Cornell

I hung up the phone and sobbed. Loss! Terrible heart-breaking loss. This was the death of someone I love very much, but the person was still alive. It was the death of our connection.

Sometimes in life, we have to make very hard choices as to whether or not it is healthy to carry on a relationship. The two of us mutually made a choice to not carry on, because it was causing too much pain for both of us. I made the decision out of love, but I wasn't even sure of all of the reasons why this had happened! There is still an emptiness, a void in my heart, that can never ever be filled. How could this happen? I had examined my own heart, asked forgiveness for what I had contributed to the situation, and prayed for the other. Where was God in all of this? Have you ever had to sever a relationship or have it severed for you? This can happen for many reasons, but the result is the same. Unbearable loss!

I knelt in prayer. *"Heavenly Father, God of all love and mercy. You know our hearts. You know that deep in my soul, I would never want this to happen. You know the whole story of what has brought this to be, which I don't fully understand. I pray You are with this one I love. Touch their soul. Be with them in a mighty way, Lord, and give them peace. I thank you, Lord, for this loved one. I pray they have a good life and depend on you. Perhaps one day, heal this relationship to the place You would want us to be. I ask this in Jesus' name. Amen."*

I woke up the next morning. Was there a bit of freedom I was feeling? Free from worry. Free from guilt. I was still heartbroken, but God had given me peace, wonderful peace. Oh, the love of God! He was in control of this. I continue in this peace to this day.

There is terrible grief in the loss of one who is still alive, but in the midst of it is the song of joy in my heart, *Wonderful Peace.*

> *Peace peace wonderful peace, coming down from the Father above.*
> *Sweep over my spirit forever I pray in fathomless billows of love.*[45]

God loves me so much that he has given me peace in the midst of my grief! Thank you, Lord Jesus!

~~~~~~~~~~~~~~~~~~~~~~~~~~~~

LET'S TALK ABOUT GOD'S PEACE:

Loss in your life! These are the things we all experience. Have you ever experienced loss in having to step away from someone you

---

[45] Cornell, Warren D. (Words), William G. Cooper (Music), Copyright © 1889, "Wonderful Peace", in the Public Domain.

love? No matter what you have tried, there doesn't seem to be a way to find a middle ground? Have you been hurt by someone who has walked away from you? There is no greater hurt than losing a person you love who is still alive. It could be a family member or a very good friend. So many have told me stories of parents separated from an adult child, siblings not talking to each other, grandparents unable to see their grandchildren, or great friends separated by misunderstandings or disagreements, etc. But, as long as that person is still alive, there is hope. In that hope, the Holy Spirit can help you find joy in that deep down peace that only he can give. Perhaps you have not lost someone, but there is always tension when you are together. From the Bible:

> Do not be anxious about anything, but in every situation, by prayer and petition, with thanksgiving, present your requests to God. And the peace of God, which transcends all understanding, will guard your hearts and your minds in Christ Jesus.
>
> **Philippians 4:6-7 (NIV)**

Paul wrote this letter to the Philippian church which had started with a motley crew of believers. Paul and Silas were in prison there, and it was looking bad for them. They were flogged and put in a dingy cell with mud for floors, no toilets, and life looked hopeless, but what did they do? There they were, on their knees thanking and praising God at that very lowest time of their lives. God provided an earthquake which broke open the cell door. The prison guard's life was changed by God and the miracle he had just witnessed. Other prisoners and their families escaped and along with the jailer became the first Philippian church.

I love that in prayer with <u>thanksgiving</u>, God will guard our hearts and minds.

In many circumstances, it may be difficult to even <u>think</u> about thanking and praising God, but God is in control. Pray like Paul and Silas in your terrible times, thanking God for Who He is and for what He will do in your life. If you have this type of loss or tension, I realize this is terribly hard for you.

Life will be different, but God will be with you in this awful experience. Every day the Holy Spirit will offer you peace and the fruits of the spirit will become evident and working in your life.

> But the fruit of the Spirit is love, joy, peace, forbearance, kindness, goodness, faithfulness, gentleness, and self-control. Against such things there is no law.
>
> **Galatians 5:22-23 (NIV)**

KEY TO FINDING GOD'S JOY #19:

Even in the most difficult times of loss in your life, look through the darkness of pain to see the light of God. Know that God is with you through it all, even in the darkest of dark times. If someone is separated from you, pray for both of you. If there is tension between you and another, pray for both of you. God loves that person. God will give you peace and deep-down joy in the midst of the pain when you know God is love and you see the person in that light. God will give you peace and joy amidst any crisis in your life if you go to Him.

PRAYERFULLY THINK ABOUT YOUR OWN LIFE WITH GOD:

Are you separated from someone you love? It is up to us to open our hearts and look around to begin showing the fruits of the Spirit. Opening yourself to the needs of others can be a way for God to begin to heal your wounds and bring these fruits. Slowly, acceptance of the reality will come. This process will never be easy. God will bring you through it.

Where is God's peace? He wants to give it to you wherever you are. We do not need to look in remote places or circumstances to find His peace. In the end, it is necessary for us all to understand that the gift of God's peace is given to you where you are, when you are ready for it, and when you want it. Will you surrender your will and your life into the care and keeping of God? It is in that surrender that perhaps the first words of gratitude to God and praise to God in the circumstance can finally come to your mind and mouth. Then there will be God's healing peace and joy.

Perhaps you haven't been totally separated from someone you love, but there is always tension in the air when you are together. Will you give this also to God? He is in control. Search your own heart to make sure you have not hurt the other. Pray. Ask forgiveness if you have hurt them. If you are in these circumstances, are you ready to surrender and receive peace? Write a few of your thoughts. I know there can be hurt. God knows your hurt.

_____

_____

_____

_____

_____

_____

_____

_____

A Song of God's Comfort

I'm possessed of a hope that is steadfast and sure
Since Jesus came into my heart
And no dark clouds of doubt now my pathway obscure
Since Jesus came into my heart.
- Rufus H. McDaniel and
Charles Hutchinson Gabriel

*T*here is great pain in the death of a relative or very close friend. After Mom's fall and hip replacement in 2018, a neck doctor talked with Mom, David, and me when Mom couldn't regain her ability to hold herself up on a walker.

"Your mom's spinal cord is squashed in her neck. Without surgery, she will never walk again. The nerve pain will get so bad that not even morphine will completely cover it."

Mom did not want any more surgery. I left the room and cried. Mom survived with that pain and morphine for three long years in the nursing home. She went home to be with the Lord in 2021.

Now there was another huge hole in my heart. Before her death, we had talked twice a day and I had visited her many times a week. We survived the time of the Covid 19 pandemic in 2020 and 2021 when

I was not allowed to visit. The nurse brought Mom to the 3rd-floor lounge window. I was on the ground below whether snow or rain or sunny weather. They would connect us through FaceTime so we could see each other closely and talk, but Mom could also see me in person on the ground below. Sometimes, the activity coordinator rolled a keyboard over to the window, so Mom could play by ear and serenade me. Windows were open in all seasons, so the music of hymns and other songs could float down to my ears. Beautiful sounds of my mom's last talent. Other times we would use FaceTime from my home to the nursing home.

One day on FaceTime, Mom looked beside her on the bed and said, "Who's this little pumpkin?"

"What little pumpkin, Mom?"

"It's a beautiful baby boy. The most beautiful baby I have ever seen. What is he doing here next to me?

"Is it one of the dolls from the nursing home, Mom?"

"No. He's not a doll. Who left him here? Someone should come and get him." Mom then closed her eyes. That was the last mention of the baby.

A couple of days later and about 4 months before Mom died, the hospice nurse called, "I think you should come in. We may be close to your Mom's time."

My weak mom spoke when David and I got there. "Jesus visited me yesterday. He told me he is waiting for me but I don't have to rush. What would a person do if they didn't know Jesus was waiting for them?"

"I think they would be scared," I said. "I know I couldn't handle it if I didn't know you were going to be with the Lord." Mom wasn't eating or drinking and had lost much weight.

My brother, his wife, and one of their daughters joined us through FaceTime as did our sons and their families. We just couldn't get ahold of my brother's other daughter and her husband, and I left a message for them.

The next day Mom's granddaughter called her. Even though she hadn't planned on telling anyone until she was further along, she said, "Grandma, we are expecting a baby."

"Do you know if it is a boy or girl yet?" asked Mom.

"Not yet, but I will let you know when I do." They talked for a long time. "I love you, Grandma!"

Do you know what my mom did? Jesus had said there was no rush. That very day she ate half of an egg. The next day she had two eggs and a piece of toast. She was going to see her great-grandbaby! Her pastor said that sometimes God gives visions to the old. She so wanted to see that baby. Maybe God had already shown her the new baby coming to the family. I told my niece that Mom had seen a baby boy next to her in bed.

Weeks later she texted me with the news.

"We're having a boy, Aunt Susan. Maybe Grandma really saw our baby."

Mom cried. My mom did not live long enough to see that new great-grandson in person, but I like to think God let her see him that day before he was ever born.

During the four months before my mom died, we had more good talks. I told her that I had heard someone talk about when your loved one dies. This person had said that we are saying goodbye and crying, but all those waiting for her in Heaven, including our Lord, would be saying, "Look! Here she comes!" That made Mom giggle. She said I would have to include that story in my eulogy. She couldn't wait to be with Jesus. That gave me comfort.

Two weeks before Mom died, I went into the hospital with multiple blood clots in my lungs, and I was there for a week.

"Should I tell Mom I'm in the hospital?" I asked her nurse.

"She can take it. Don't you want her prayers?"

My mom always said, "When I go to be with the Lord, my prayers for you and your brother and your families will all be written in Heaven."

I told her about the clots, and we talked every day while I was in the hospital. She handled it well. When I returned home, I was supposed to stay still for some days and rest. It was the next Wednesday when David finally pushed me into her room in a wheelchair. "Your mom is sleeping," said her nurse. "Cecile. Susan is here."

Mom opened her eyes, but she didn't look at me. She raised her arms to Heaven and over and over I heard her joy. "Thank you, Jesus. Thank you, Jesus. Thank you, Lord Jesus!"

I believe she had been asking God to help her hang on until she could see me again. What a great talk we had! I had told my brother and his wife from Michigan the day and time we were going, so they called on my phone where I could turn on the speaker.

"We love you, Mom!" they both said. Mom thought we were all in the room together. She was filled with the joy of the Lord.

She kept saying to all of us, "I love you so much. More than you know. God will take care of you." What joy and comfort she had that day!

Mom went home to the Lord the following Saturday. David and I were with her that day. Praise God that she is at peace in her new home with God in Heaven. The Lord gave me comfort in the old song, *Since Jesus Came into My Heart.*

> *There's a light in the valley of death now for me since Jesus came into my heart. And the gates of the city beyond I can see, since Jesus came into my heart. Since Jesus came into my heart.*
> *Since Jesus came into my heart. Floods of joy o'er my soul like the sea billows roll, since Jesus came into my heart.*[46]

I have peace over the loss of my dad and mom whom I know I will see again in Heaven. That gives me comfort and joy.

~~~~~~~~~~~~~~~~~~~~~~~~~~~~~~~

LET'S TALK ABOUT GOD'S COMFORT:

In our grief over the loss of a loved one, I know from my counselor that there are five stages of this grief originally denoted by Elizabeth Kubler Ross.

---

[46] McDaniel, Rufus H. and Charles Hutchinson Gabriel, Copyright © 1914, "Since Jesus Came into My Heart", in the Public Domain.

162

First is denial. I couldn't believe I had actually lost my dad or mom in death.

The second is anger. I seem to have a problem with feeling the anger part. I have never felt very angry about anything, but some counseling has helped me realize that stuffing anger down can only make you sick and I have had much sickness! I am working on taking walks and just calmly telling God times that have made me angry. You don't have to yell when you are angry, although many do. You just have to get it out.

The third is bargaining. I did this. *"What could I have done differently, Lord? If only I could have kept Mom from falling."*

The fourth stage is depression. It is natural to feel depressed after a loss. It is the true deep-down grieving of our loss in life, knowing the loved one will never come back to be with us.

The final stage is acceptance. This does not mean your loss is not felt. It may never be O.K. to have the loss in your life forever. Acceptance is more about knowing the reality of the situation and giving it over to God. God is in control, and He will get you through this. He will comfort you.

The sudden death of a loved one can feel almost impossible to handle. I have a dear friend, Melissa, whose son died of a drug overdose. He had been going to church and trying so hard to come off drugs and alcohol. Melissa said goodnight to him the day before his birthday. During the night, he was tempted and made a terrible choice. He was actually killed by the drug supplier who left him and did not get help for him in her rush to get rid of the evidence. She was convicted of homicide. At her sentencing, Melissa was allowed to tell this woman how her son's death had affected her and the family. As a Christian, Melissa also told her that she loved and forgave her. In times such as this, there is no understanding. These are the times when every day, one must cling to God to help you make it through the day. These are the days when you cling to your friends to pray for you as you go through the denial and anger stages, since it is almost impossible for you to pray. Life at this point makes no sense and all the questions come. Where was God in this?

We do know that God is with those who have been faithful. Death will not separate our loved ones or us from the care of God.

> ...Be faithful until death, and I will give you the crown of life.
>
> **Revelation 2:10 (NASB)**

KEY TO FINDING GOD'S JOY #20:

Rest in God's arms when you experience the death of a loved one. He is the only one who can bring you peace and a joy deep down that your loved one is no longer suffering. If the death has been sudden, it is a terrible shock to you. There is nothing in human life that can help us with that immediate loss. It will take time for you to work through the stages of grief. Only God can help you to make it through each day. Begin each day one step at a time, giving each painful moment to God. Pray for His comfort and a peace that passes all understanding. I pray you will be able to receive it and slowly find joy in your life again.

PRAYERFULLY THINK ABOUT YOUR OWN LIFE WITH GOD:

Do not rush but breathe in the peace that only God can give in these hard losses. Look around you to see God's goodness and the gifts of the Spirit which are there for you. Then, begin to give those fruits of the Spirit to others. Can you think about helping others in need?

Give of yourself. If you are in the midst of your pain in loss, this may all seem like "pie in the sky" theology. Do not underestimate the power of God. He is there with you. He will not leave you. Focusing on someone else may help you see God's power at work. God loves you and wants to give you His joy and His peace. If you have a loss, what stage are you in now, and how will you move to acceptance? Get your feelings out on this page. God wants to know your innermost thoughts whether it be denial, anger, bargaining, depression, or acceptance. If you haven't experienced loss in your life yet, what have you thought about here that may help you in future losses? Unfortunately, there will be loss for everyone.

_____

_____

_____

_____

_____

_____

_____

_____

_____

_____

_____

_____

_____

_____

A Song of God's Intricate Creation

Let all things their Creator bless,
And worship Him in humbleness.
O praise Him! Alleluia!
St. Francis of Assisi translated by William Draper
- Ralph Vaughn Williams

There I was sitting in my chair again. I didn't want to move or do anything around the house. I didn't want to get exercise or go outside. I just felt sad and wanted to sit. Have you ever felt like that?

After the blood clots and the death of my dear mother two weeks later, I realized that I was also dealing with depression and perhaps had been for a while. I prayed about it, but the desire to sit in "my" chair and do nothing was overwhelming. My rheumatologist suggested I start with a Christian counselor. Even today as I write this, it is hard to admit that giving it all to God and praying just wasn't taking away the symptoms. These thoughts were in my head. *"God, I have prayed for the lifting of this desire to do nothing. I know You are there. Have I let You down now? Come Holy Spirit."* Through a test, my counselor found I had severe depression and anxiety. She sent me to my doctor.

We have all experienced some form of sadness and depression in our lives. It is part of living in this world. When I realized my test showed severe depression and anxiety, I thought I had failed in some way in my relationship with God. There feels like there is a stigma to a Christian not being able to get rid of their own depression. Please read on to what I have discovered. Through my doctor, I realized that I had a disease. It was not my fault. It was like getting cancer or blood clots. My doctor took the time to teach me.

"Explain this to me," I said. "Does depression come from the events of your life and shouldn't you be able to shake it off through prayer or is it a disease that just comes?"

"It can be both. Some people are born with the inability of the brain to make enough serotonin. That is the chemical in your brain that makes you feel better. Those people have problems with depression early in life. Others have continuing problems or diseases over a long period of time like you, Susan. With each problem or trying to get over a disease, the serotonin in the brain gets depleted and the brain has to make more. After such a long time of doing this over the past many years with the problems you have had, the brain just can't keep up with the serotonin needs. Then you can suffer from depression. That is what has happened to you. That is when you may need some serotonin replaced medically. This is a disease."

It is awesome how complicated our bodies are and how they can be often healed when we are sick. Through the help of my doctor and counselor and with the prayers of my family and friends, I am back to feeling much better. What a blessing that God has given us doctors to help us through our health needs. I thank God for friends who understand, stand with you, and pray for you as you go through these times. As I look back on the past years of pain and disease, I can only thank God that He has brought refuge and hope and His help through each trial. He has created amazing bodies for us! He has also created a wonderfully complex world where we can find peace and joy in the midst of our pain. Praise God!

> *All creatures of our God and King; lift up your voice and with us sing.*
> *Alleluia! Alleluia! Thou burning sun with golden beam; Thou silver moon with softer gleam. O praise Him, O praise Him.*
> *Alleluia! Alleluia! Alleluia!*[47]

~~~~~~~~~~~~~~~~~~~~~~~~~~~~~~~~~~~~~

LET'S TALK ABOUT GOD'S INTRICATE CREATION:

Our Creator made our bodies very complicated. It is amazing how all the parts work in harmony to keep us alive. It is even more amazing what the brain does to control all of our movement and thinking, that which we realize and that which is automatically controlled. The balance of hormones in the brain is what keeps us from depression. How can one think of the intricacies of our bodies and of all of nature and not believe there is a Creator who figured it all out for the world?

> For You created my inmost being; You knit me together in my mother's womb. I praise You because I am fearfully and wonderfully made; Your works are wonderful, I know that full well.
>
> **Psalm 139:13-14 (NIV)**

---

[47] St. Francis of Assisi, 1182–1226 (Words), trans. by William H. Draper, Copyright © 1919, "All Creatures of Our God and King", in the Public Domain, Ralph Vaughan Williams (Music arr.), Copyright ©1906, arranged from 'Lasst Uns Erfreuen' from Geistliche Kirchengesäng Köln, (Music) Copyright © 1623, in the Public Domain.

God as Creator is being proven through science. Mitochondria are parts in every cell of a human that carry a small amount of DNA. Mitochondria come to us through the mother. Mothers pass their mitochondrial DNA to both their daughters and sons. Fathers do not pass mitochondrial DNA (mtDNA). The mtDNA of the descendants from any female lineage and that of all the lineages divide the human population into various haplogroups. However, the variations in the mitochondrial DNA resulting from mutations in the DNA between people have conclusively shown that all people have descended from one female, just as the Bible states. Scientists call that one female "Eve".

I learned this when I tested my DNA through Family Tree DNA. If you do your own DNA test including the mtDNA sequence (mitochondrial DNA), it will tell your haplogroup from which you descended and how the path came from Eve's location in Africa (thousands of years ago) to where your more recent ancestors have lived. Other haplogroups go out in different directions across the world from the original Eve. Family Tree DNA even gives you maps to follow your haplogroup from Eve to where your more recent ancestors were living. It is really quite amazing how the genome process of identification has led us to one family that started it all. Science is amazing! The Creator is amazing! We are all part of one family!

In my depression, I learned much about my body. I had an imbalance. I also learned that God is there working through doctors and counselors who will help us, and He works through the prayers of many. I could still sense the joy in my soul that God has given me, because He is there. It is a sureness! Hallelujah!

Sometimes, as Christians, we don't want to admit that we are depressed. It seems like God should be able to take it away. But I have had so many tell me "thank you" for opening up about it and sharing. Perhaps someday, my testimony of getting through depression with doctors and medicine, my counselor, prayers of my faithful friends at church in Bible study, many others, and God will help someone else seek help too. Depression can be a deadly disease.

> When anxiety was great within me,
> Your consolation brought me joy.
>
> **Psalm 94:19 (NIV)**

KEY TO FINDING GOD'S JOY #21:

Not only has God created us in an amazing way but also the world and the universe. He is worthy to be praised! He has created the ways here on earth for us to be healed of many diseases including depression. Find your rest and joy in the knowledge that He is with you when you are having problems with health including depression. God knows your name. He knows what you are experiencing. Ask and He will provide help. Don't wait! (I am not suggesting here that all diseases can be cured. God is there for you whether there is a cure or not. He may heal you in a moment. Or your help may come in a form of peace and joy in your soul from God, since our bodies will all die of some disease.)

PRAYERFULLY THINK ABOUT YOUR OWN LIFE WITH GOD:

There isn't one among us who does not have a need in our lives, and Jesus can bring us through it. Have you thought about the intricacies of your body? How does it all keep functioning? Did you realize that science has brought us to the point of realizing that we all came from one mother, Eve? God's creation is something great to behold. Have you had any experience with depression? As a Christian, were you embarrassed to admit that to anyone? God doesn't want that for you.

He wants to help you heal. If you have depression, write about it now and what you are going to do to seek help. If you do not have depression, take some time here to write down all the gifts we have in God's creation including the intricacies of your own body. They are abundant!!

_____

_____

_____

_____

_____

_____

_____

_____

_____

_____

_____

_____

_____

_____

_____

_____

_____

_____

A Song of God's Encouragement

Gushing from the Rock before me,
Lo a spring of joy I see!
- Fanny Crosby and Robert Lowry

"I don't think I can step out this door, David. I can't be away from you overnight. I want to go, but I don't want to walk out the door."

I thought back to how all of this had started. Barb had seen my depression, was with me through it, and was seeing me come out of it. She had a great idea. Calling me on the phone, she proposed a fun outing. "What would you think about going with Linda and Beverly and me to Galena, IL? We could stay overnight at a beautiful ski resort. On Friday, we'll drive to Dubuque, Iowa to board a riverboat for a leisurely trip up the Mississippi and back. It'll be fun and relaxing! You need some fun, Susan."

Linda and Beverly are Barb's sisters and therefore my "sisters". "I will have to think about it a bit," I said. Eventually, I called Barb back and said, "Let's do it! I've been sitting in my depression chair for too long!"

"Great!" she said. "I'll plan it all and let you know the cost. This is going to be great!"

Barb was encouraging me to leave the safety of my chair at home and take a step toward freedom. She was counting on God to help me do it. I felt that God was also encouraging me to step out of my cocoon caused by the depression. He didn't want to see me in this state. He wanted to heal me from the depression and bring happiness and joy into my life again. Deep down in my soul, even in the worst of the depression, I still felt the joy of the Lord in my heart telling me that He was with me. He would get me through it. Sometimes, I wasn't sure how. The counselor and the medicine from my doctor were certainly helping me. I thanked God for them each day. However, I had not yet stepped out of my safe place at home.

The day came to leave on our adventure. I reluctantly packed my little bag for the trip. *"God. Can I do this?"* As I went to the door to leave, I felt a strong pull to stay at home.

David encouraged me. "You're going with Barb, Linda, and Beverly! They're like sisters to you. You're going to be fine. God will take care of you, and I bet you'll have the greatest time. You can do this, Suz. Don't forget I love you!"

"Pray for me, David," I said as I took the step through the doorway.

That step was all it took. The four of us were on our way to Galena, IL. We talked and laughed all the way. Barb had made goodie bags for each of us for the trip with snacks and lotion. Our hotel was beautiful, and we enjoyed dinner on the balcony overlooking the Mississippi. The sunset was glorious. Peace was settling in my soul.

"O.K. Everyone ready for some real fun?" asked Barb. She had a game on her phone which was like Password. You held the phone on your forehead. That alone looked hilarious. Then, the timer would start and everyone would start giving you clues as to what word was sitting there atop your head. If you got the word, you tilted the phone up from your forehead. If you gave up, you tilted it down. Whoever got the most words correct in the time limit won the round. Sitting in the hotel room on beds or chairs, my sides were about to split from all the laughing. Crazy clues, wrong answers, and the phone going up and down on the foreheads were enough to make us laugh all night long. I was actually having fun!

After driving to Dubuque the next morning, we boarded the riverboat for our Mississippi adventure. The trip up the river was filled with the captain giving us the history of the area along with breakfast and lunch. The trip back down the river to our dock was filled with snacks and with music. A man who played the guitar, ukulele, and the harmonica sang indoors, but it was piped all over the boat. As the four of us sat on the side deck of the boat watching the river and scenery, we sang along with all the songs he was singing - songs from childhood, favorite songs from past days, hymns, and silly songs. Joy was overflowing in my heart as we sang "Somewhere Over the Rainbow/What a Wonderful World"[48] made famous by Israel Kamakawiwo'ole!

God brought me through this trip in a mighty way. I did not feel depressed. I did not miss sitting in my depression chair. I had a peace which passes all understanding. There was such encouragement through my friends and through our powerful God!

I am reminded of a hymn as I write: *All the Way My Savior Leads Me.*

---

[48] Arlen, Harold, Yip Harburg, Bog thiele, and George Daavid Weiss, Copyright © 1990, (Israel Kamakawiwo'ole) Big Boy Records: New Orleans, Louisiana.

All the way my Savior leads me; What have I to ask beside? Can I doubt His tender mercy, who through life has been my Guide? Heav'nly peace, divinest comfort here by faith in Him to dwell; For I know whate'er befall me, Jesus doeth all things well. For I know whate'er befall me, Jesus doeth all things well. All the way my Savior leads me, cheers each winding path I tread, gives me grace for ev'ry trial, feeds me with the living bread. Though my weary steps may falter and my soul athirst may be; Gushing from the Rock before me, lo a spring of joy I see. Gushing from the Rock before me, lo a spring of joy I see.[49]

~~~~~~~~~~~~~~~~~~~~~~~~~~~~~~~

LET'S TALK ABOUT GOD'S ENCOURAGEMENT:

God has given us a wonderful world with friends to stand with us in trouble, to love us, and to encourage us along our way through this life. When do we need to be encouraged? You need courage when you fear. How many times did Jesus tell his disciples, "Do not fear"? How we need friends to come alongside of us and remind us not to fear. People from church can be encouragers. If you don't have close friends, join or become more involved in your church.

God himself is also the great encourager. Paul wrote to the church in Thessalonica:

> So then, brothers and sisters, stand firm and hold to the teachings we passed on to you, whether by word of mouth or by letter. May our Lord Jesus Christ Himself

---

[49] Crosby, Frances Jane (Fanny) (words) and Robert Lowry (music), Copyright © 1875, "All the Way My Savior Leads Me", in the Public Domain.

and God our Father, who loved us and by His grace gave us eternal encouragement and good hope, encourage your hearts and strengthen you in every good deed and word.

2 Thessalonians 2:15-17 (NIV)

God finds ways through friends, through reading His word in the Bible, and through prayer or miracles to encourage us along our journey. He also asks us to encourage others. Once again in his letter to the Thessalonians, Paul spoke of this:

...Live in peace with each other. And we urge you, brothers and sisters, warn those who are idle and disruptive, encourage the disheartened, help the weak, be patient with everyone. Make sure that nobody pays back wrong for wrong, but always strive to do what is good for each other and for everyone else.

1 Thessalonians 5:13-15 (NIV)

KEY TO FINDING GOD'S JOY #22:

In your tough times, allow the encouragement of others into your life. It can make such a difference for the good. Also, know that God is encouraging you in all you do. Find joy and peace in knowing that He is with you, encouraging you to move forward in His will for your life.

PRAYERFULLY THINK ABOUT YOUR OWN LIFE WITH GOD:

God gives us encouragement and hope! Are you in a time when you have lost hope? What has brought that into your life? Have you had an earlier time when you lost hope? When was that? How did you come out of it? Did someone encourage you? Did someone kindly kick you in the pants and say, "Let's do this!"?

Did you find encouragement from God through His word or through His work in your life? Did you find encouragement from a sermon or in looking around you to see all the gifts that God has provided in your life? Perhaps you haven't yet found that hope and encouragement. After reading this, what can you do to help yourself see the encouragement that God wants to give you? God wants your life to be all it can be through Him. Think about a time that you were encouraged by others or by God. I am encouraging you right now if you feel hopeless. God is there for you. Take a few moments to write about God's encouragement in your life.

_____

_____

_____

_____

_____

_____

_____

_____

_____

_____

_____

_____

_____

_____

_____

A Song of God's Presence

His eye is on the sparrow
And I know He watches me.
- Civilla Durfee Martin and
Charles Hutchinson Gabriel

Has someone in your life hurt you in such a way that you thought you might never recover?

I cried out to God. "Why this? Why me? What can I do to heal this? What can I do to help this person?"

Every night, I tossed and turned and wrestled with myself and God in bed. *"What should I do? Take away this hurt, Lord. Is there something I can do to change this, Lord?"* Tears flowed on my pillow. My heart hurt that someone could do something so undeserved by me.

God gave me two words over and over again. *"LOVE and FORGIVE, Susan."* And yet He was not yet finished with how He would work in me and through others in this situation.

I prayed for this person. I do not say that to pat myself on the back. I feel sorrow for this person. God has taught me that love, forgiveness, and focusing on leaving that person in God's hands is the only way to peace.

> *"My God. I thank you and praise you! You are my Lord and Savior. Thank You for all You have done in my life and in my heart. Thank You for your song still in my soul. I need You. I need to feel Your mighty presence in my life. I cannot deal with this by myself, Lord. I turn this all over to You. Give me peace and joy in the midst of this pain. I thank You now for what You will do to help me get through this time. Help me with forgiving and loving and help me to know if there is something I have done that I haven't asked forgiveness for from _____. Be with this child of Yours in a mighty way. Help them to see you. You are in control. Amen."*

This situation has never been resolved, and it may never be. It is something about God and my prayers that I do not understand, but I have to leave it in God's hands. Perhaps His lesson is for me to leave it with Him and have faith. We do not always get answers to our problems in the way we would like to see them resolved.

This event crushed me at the time, but God had plans to make His presence known to me in ways greater than I could ever imagine. Blessings rained down on me like refreshing showers.

"Hi Susan. This is Sonia." She was my mom's best friend's daughter. "Since our moms have been best friends and 'sisters', I want to become your sister in Christ. I've been helping get groceries or doing some chores for a lady who is 101. She has a favorite daily devotional that she reads. I thought that I would get a copy for you and for me. We can read it each day and be connected in the Lord through that devotion." That is Sonia. She answers God's call to love one another in many ways.

"Oh Sonia! I would love that! Each day, we will be reading the same words about the Lord, and each day we will be also thinking about and praying for each other!"

The devotional book came in the mail that August. The book was Paul David Tripp's book, *New Morning Mercies: A Daily Gospel Devotional*. I read my first devotion for the day, and I couldn't even believe what God was communicating that day.

"August 4 *When nothing else or no one else in your life remains and is faithful, you can rest assured that God will be both.*" Stunned, I read on as the devotion talked about the honesty of the Bible and how it didn't play "monkey games with reality". It focused on Psalm 90 and difficulties in life. "Every day is marked by little troubles, and big trouble will enter your door as well... If you are God's child, you are not alone. Glorious grace has connected you to the One whose power and love don't shift with the times. Grace has connected you to the One who is the ultimate dwelling place... This means I am never left just to my own resources. I am never left to figure out and deal with life on my own... Grace has opened the door of hope and refuge to me by connecting me to One who is eternal and who rules all circumstances and relationships that would cause me to feel alone."[50]

> *"Wow! Thank you, God, for that word of reassurance that you are present and with me throughout my life, whatever I am going through at the time!"*

God was still not finished with showing me His presence and His love. A few days later, a letter came in an email from a woman of God who has been a friend for years. Mickie has ministered to

---

[50] Taken from *New Morning Mercies: A Daily Gospel Devotional* by Paul David Tripp, Copyright © 2014, p. August 4. Used by permission of Crossway, a publishing ministry of Good News Publishers, Wheaton, IL 60187, www.crossway.org.

Christians in India, and she has been consulting with churches around the U.S. She is also the chaplain for a motorcycle club. Quite an interesting friend. She had felt led to send me a note at that time. Part of it was directly from God.

"I'm not normally very charismatic, but I have prayed for you today. I sense the Lord telling me to encourage you with some specific words. This is what the Lord wants you to know: "*You have done nothing wrong. Something has been killing you... Lean back into your Father's arms. Breathe out the poison you have been carrying. Breathe in deep, refreshing, renewed breaths of life.*""

Wow again! Now I was humbled. God was with me. He was present. This is why we forgive.

The poison of hatred or anger or resentment cannot help us in life. God can renew your life in the midst of the pain and remind you of the joy in your heart.

Amazing grace! This was a second direct word from God for me. God brought to my mind the old hymn often sung in the past by Ethel Waters, *His Eye Is On The Sparrow*.

> *Why should I feel discouraged, Why should the shadows come, Why should my heart be lonely, And long for heav'n and home, when Jesus is my portion? My constant friend is He: His eye is on the sparrow, and I know He watches me; His eye is on the sparrow, and I know He watches me. I sing because I'm happy. I sing because I'm free. For His eye is on the sparrow, and I know He watches me. Whenever I am tempted, Whenever clouds arise, When songs give place to sighing, When hope within me dies, I draw the closer to Him, From care He set me free; His eye is on the*

sparrow, And I know He watches me; His eye is on the sparrow, And I know He watches me. I sing because I'm happy. I sing because I'm free. For His eye is on the sparrow, and I know He watches me.[51]

How could I ever worry again after this? I may still, but I shouldn't!

~~~~~~~~~~~~~~~~~~~~~~~~~~~~~~~~~~~~~~~

LET'S TALK ABOUT GOD'S PRESENCE:

Therefore I tell you, do not worry about your life, what you will eat or drink; or about your body, what you will wear. Is not life more important than food, and the body more than clothes? Look at the birds of the air; they do not sow or reap or store away in barns, and yet your heavenly Father feeds them. Are you not much more valuable than they? Can any one of you by worrying add a single hour to his life?

Matthew 6:25-27 (NIV)

God will help us to heal in the tough times. Praise God for this gift. We are not alone in our troubles. We can ask God to help heal our pain. It may not come soon. It may never come, but we no longer have to be downtrodden. If we need to ask for forgiveness, we do that which is right in God's eyes. If we need to forgive someone, it is not for them that we need to do it. It is for our own hearts that we do not carry pain and anger and sorrow throughout our lives. We can experience joy again in the peace that God gives us. He is in control.

---

[51] Martin, Civilla Dufee (words) and Charles H. Gabriel (music), Copyright © 1905, "His Eye Is On The Sparrow", [Ethel Waters], in the Public Domain.

God has been this ever-present help throughout my life. His presence is always there. I realize that God does not always bring such miraculous mercies when life is tough. These were extraordinary days in the wake of heart-breaking days.

There have also been many times when I wondered if God was truly present with me. After I first accepted the Lord and was filled with his joy and the Holy Spirit, I eventually came down from the mountain. These times are when our faith grows, and God sees we are devoted to him. As disease after disease came, I sometimes wondered if He was truly there, and I wanted to feel His presence with me. Notice the word "feel". I wanted the feeling that He was there, not just the knowledge and faith.

Oswald Chambers said something very wise about feelings and faith. "If we continually try to bring back those exceptional moments of inspiration, it is a sign that it is not God we want. We are becoming obsessed with the moments when God did come and speak with us, and we are insisting that He do it again. But what God wants us to do is to 'walk by faith'... Then comes our surprise and we find ourselves exclaiming, 'Why, He was there all the time, and I never knew it.' Never live for those exceptional moments – they are surprises."[52]

You may be thinking to yourself... *"What is God's role in the unfolding of my daily life?"* My friend, Claire, gave me permission to share about her faith. She described her journey as having those close emotional encounters with God but then having times when nothing big was happening. She didn't feel a closeness to God. She told me that this is when your faith really kicks in to help you

---

[52] Taken from *My Utmost for His Highest* by Oswald Chambers, edited by James Reimann, © 1992 by Oswald Chambers Publications Assn., Ltd., "Faith.. Not Emotion", Entry May 1, and used by permission of Our Daily Bread Publishing, Grand Rapids MI 49501. All rights reserved.

through those times when you don't feel as close to God as you have been in the past. You continue in faith knowing God is there. It is not an emotional connection with God at that time. It is pure faith that He is with you.

And then out of nowhere, God is there in a powerful way, and you KNOW. You feel His presence. Things change like the seasons.

My friend, Rose, posted this thought of hers on Facebook. (I asked Rose's permission to print it here.) "It's amazing to watch the transformation of a tree as summer fades to autumn, just as the Holy Spirit fills us and old things fall away as we are made new. In our winter season, there may be pain as our souls are laid bare. But then, yes then, spring arrives and we are born again, and changed, bearing new fruit. God has to help us shed old habits and beliefs many times during the process of our sanctification."

Yes. Our Lord leads us through many times of growth and change and doubt and pain, but He truly is always present with us. God is helping us to grow throughout our lives whether we feel His presence at any particular moment or not.

> In all this you greatly rejoice, though now for a little while you may have had to suffer grief in all kinds of trials. These have come so that the proven genuineness of your faith - of greater worth than gold, which perishes even though refined by fire - may result in praise, glory and honor when Jesus Christ is revealed. Though you have not seen Him, you love Him; and even though you do not see Him now, you believe in Him and are filled with an inexpressible and glorious joy.
>
> **1 Peter 1:6-8 (NIV)**

Blessed are those who have learned to acclaim You, who walk in the light of Your presence, Lord. They rejoice in Your name all day long; they celebrate Your righteousness.

Psalm 89:15-16 (NIV)

KEY TO FINDING GOD'S JOY # 23:

When hurt, forgive the person who has hurt you. Make sure that you have asked forgiveness for anything you may have done. Know that God is present with you whether you feel Him or not. Let your faith sustain you when you do not feel His presence. God is there! Sometimes be amazed and filled with joy by the miracles He works to show you His presence!

PRAYERFULLY THINK ABOUT YOUR OWN LIFE WITH GOD:

If you know Jesus as your Lord and Savior, He has sent the Holy Spirit to dwell within you at all times. Do you need to forgive someone for an unbearable hurt? Give it over to the Holy Spirit to transform your mind and free you from the hurt. Forgive them.

Do you need to ask for forgiveness? The Spirit teaches us and helps us to grow. Perhaps not "feeling" God there at times is a way for the Spirit of God to help grow our faith. We then step out in faith, knowing that God's word is true and that He is with us to the ends of the earth. Have you had a time in your life when you truly sensed the Lord carrying you and getting you through a struggle? What happened? Did you feel His peace? Maybe you are going through that right now.

Have you experienced times when it didn't feel like God was with you and you were on your own in this world? How did that feel?

Were you able to have faith that God was there no matter how you felt? Did you realize later that God had been carrying you through the darkness? Do you really need the presence of the Lord now? Do you realize He is there all the time? Take some time to reflect on God's presence in your life.

A Song of God's Faithfulness

With my mouth I will make known Thy faithfulness.
- James H. Fillmore

*W*hen I decided I wanted to write this book, I joined a Christian writing group on Zoom. I had already started this book, but I am always anxious to learn more about writing. Sharing with other Christians during this process seemed like a wonderful way to continue. There were people in the group from around the world, and our leader, Sue, was in England. In one of the first sessions, she suggested we might like to find someone in the group who was writing something similar to us and to partner up to give each other feedback. God immediately drew me to Teri. We have shared back and forth professionally and have been so thankful for each other's input. We haven't shared much about our personal lives except for a few memoir examples. She knew nothing of my illnesses or losses or depression.

I asked Teri if I could share a bit of our friendship in this book. I was texting very recently with Teri, and I said I would see her on Wednesday for our writing group. She was ready to get off the phone but hesitated. She asked me if everything was O.K. and informed me that the Holy Spirit had prompted her to stay on the phone. I let her know about some of the things going on in my life.

"You know Susan - I just felt that something was there - that you were struggling with something bigger. And God nudged me. So, to me I translate that to encourage you to know Your Father sees you and understands your fears. *"Do not be afraid Susan. For I am with you. I see you and I feel all that you feel and are worried about in this moment. You need not be afraid for you are Mine. I have called you by name. Take care. Hold fast to Me. I am your strength."* This came like a flood to me for you. He is yours and you are His."

I began to cry. In choir at church that morning, we had just sung "He Knows My Name"[53] by Tommy Walker. I said, "Teri, your word from God is exactly what I needed to hear tonight! God bless you!"

"We look to Him. He provides. I re-read the text God gave me and marveled at the goodness of God. To connect two women miles apart to encourage one another in Him. How awesome is He?"

Once again, God had revealed His incredible faithfulness to reach out to me in my needs. God has blessed me with this new friend miles away who listens to God and acts to help others like me when God nudges. Praise God for Teri and all the ways God has brought me through tough times.

It is amazing to me in this writing that a very old Sunday School song comes into my heart - *I Will Sing of the Mercies.*

> *I will sing of the mercies of the Lord forever. I will sing,*
> *I will sing.*
> *I will sing of the mercies of the Lord forever. I will sing*
> *of the mercies of the Lord.*
> *With my mouth will I make known Thy faithfulness, Thy*
> *faithfulness.*

---

[53] Walker, Tommy, Copyright © 1996, "He Knows My Name", Doulos Publishing (BMI).

With my mouth will I make known Thy faithfulness to all generations.
I will sing of the mercies of the Lord forever. I will sing of the mercies of the Lord.[54]

~~~~~~~~~~~~~~~~~~~~~~~~~~~~~~~~~

LET'S TALK ABOUT GOD'S FAITHFULNESS:

God is so faithful. He is with us in our good times and the hardest times of our lives. God nudges others to pray for us, and those prayers of others lift us up in those hard times and bring us peace. This can be true in the hardest of situations.

My friend and Bible study teacher, Linda (Barb's sister), found she had squamous cell cancer in her nose and sinuses several years ago. Now, this was one of those hardest situations to survive. She endured over twenty surgeries, reconstructions, and procedures with the cancer coming back in the midst. With the chemotherapy and the radiation, she had a lot to handle.

Linda told our Bible study that through those times she couldn't "feel" the prayers of her friends and family who were praying for her. She knew she should be feeling them and feeling the difference they made, knowing that God was working to answer her prayers and those of her friends. It was discouraging to her.

In the midst of this pain, Linda was given a vision. It was not a dream. It seemed like she was completely in the dark - a place like in outer space - darker than she had ever known. She sensed God was there. Then, she turned around in the darkness, and there were origami swans by the thousands everywhere around her floating as

---

[54] Fillmore, James. H. (words and music), Copyright unknown in 1800's, "I Will Sing of the Mercies", in the Public Domain.

far as the eye could see. They were lit from within through the darkness, all giving her peace. She knew in her heart this was God's way of showing her all of the prayers that were being said for her by family, friends, church members, and friends of friends who didn't even know her personally. God was with her! Through this vision, He chose to show her His faithfulness to be with her even when she didn't "feel" the prayers and God's hand on her. Such a fantastic God we serve.

> Know that the Lord is God. It is He who made us, and we are His; we are His people, the sheep of His pasture. Enter His gates with thanksgiving and His courts with praise; give thanks to Him and praise His name. For the Lord is good and His love endures forever; His faithfulness continues through all generations.
>
> **Psalm 100:3–5 (NIV)**

KEY TO FINDING GOD'S JOY #24:

Know that God is faithful to be with His children no matter what we are going through in our lives. He is our shepherd, always taking care of His sheep. We may not "feel" the prayers and God's response to them at times, but if we keep our faith when God seems distant when times are tough, He is there. He may even show you in a miraculous way. Hold on. God is with you bringing you joy always through all generations.

PRAYERFULLY THINK ABOUT YOUR OWN LIFE WITH GOD:

Have you wondered at times why the prayers of others for you are not felt by you? When was that in your life? Have you had a time when God really showed His faithfulness to you? What happened?

Has he brought a friend alongside of you, like Teri for me, to encourage you and give you words to bring you peace?

Can you imagine God as a shepherd trying to keep His flock of sheep together? Then one wanders off. The Bible tells us the shepherd will go to find the lost sheep. He is faithful to find us and help us when we wander or need special attention. Maybe you are "lost" right now. Has the Lord brought you back into the flock at some time in your life? You might want to reflect on that time and God's faithfulness in your life. Take a few moments to think on these questions and how they might apply to you.

_____

_____

_____

_____

_____

_____

_____

_____

_____

_____

_____

_____

_____

A Song of God's Goodness

O may this bounteous God through
all our life be near us,
With ever joyful hearts and blessed peace to cheer us.
- Martin Rinkart
(translated by Catherine Winkworth)

*D*uring this most recent period of my life, God was also working to bring me the surprise of a lifetime..

About the time Mom went into the nursing home three years before she died, I was thinking about our mother-daughter relationship and sadness again hit me about not having descendants of my own. "I have family looking backward from my life; ancestors who have preceded me," I said one day. Off went a DNA test in the mail, and eagerly I awaited the results for clues to my ancestors and relatives. The wait seemed to go on forever.

The day I received the results, I was confused. "How can this be?" Ancestry separated groups related to you by Immediate Family, Close Family, 1ˢᵗ cousin, 2ⁿᵈ cousin, 3ʳᵈ cousin, etc. My results came back with an entry under Close Family. I had never heard of this person before reading these results. This person had a family tree on Ancestry, but I knew no one on the family tree. Who was this person? How confusing! Close family can be a grandparent, aunt or uncle, nephew or niece, or half-sibling. I knew all of my grandparents, aunts and uncles, nieces, and all that was left according to age was half-sibling.

Could that be? When my matches were listed on Ancestry, a message came from a 2nd cousin I did not know. Her grandfather was my paternal grandfather's brother. I asked Marilyn if she had a person with this name on her list of relatives. This person showed as a 2nd cousin like I did on her match list. First confusion, then worries, next concern, and finally fear hit me. I knew nothing of this person. Did my dad have an affair? I knew my dad well, and he was kind and crazy about my mom. I didn't think that an affair was possible.

I looked again at the mystery person's family tree and found the mom's name. I googled her and found her obituary. Her last name was different, but the obituary listed a man who was obviously the person connected to me by the abbreviation he had as his name on Ancestry. I told Marilyn, my 2nd cousin.

"Googling! That's a great idea! I'll get started searching for clues," she said.

A bit of time passed, and Marilyn emailed me. "I found an article about a Scandinavian Stamp Collectors Club. There is a picture of the board of the organization. His name is listed as part of the board, but the people in the picture are not identified in order. Take a look at it." She sent me the link.

I went to the link and looked at the picture. I knew which one he was. He looked just like my dad!

I cropped out his picture and loaded it on my phone. Barb had been to Mom and Dad's home with me every summer for years. She knew them well. "Look who I just found a picture of, Barb," I said.

"Oh, a picture of your dad. When was it taken? His hair looks different," replied Barb.

"I don't know," I said.

Later I showed it to our son, Jason. "Look who I just found a picture of, Jas."

"Your dad?" he asked. It was clear to me that this man looked very much like my dad.

I wrote to Marilyn. "What if he isn't a nice person? What if he's a criminal?".

"How bad can he be? He is on the board of a Scandinavian Stamp Club! Message him, Susan!"

Months went by before I had the courage to message him through Ancestry. I realized by then that this person had been conceived in the late summer of 1946 after Dad returned from the navy and World War II.

At dinner for Mom's birthday, I asked, "Mom, when did you meet Dad?

"Well, we met in the choir at church in December of 1946 after the war. I think Grandma sent Dad there to meet some girls who went to church. He asked me out for our first date for New Year's Eve of 1946. We went dancing! The rest is history. We got married six months later. I sure miss your Dad!"

Mom and Dad met well after this mystery person was conceived. Whew! That gave me peace that no cheating had happened. All I had left to do was figure out how to write a tactful kind note asking if he could possibly be my half-brother. I wrote the message to him, took a deep breath, and pushed the send button.

He answered my message and said his story was quite complicated. He would email me with a longer explanation. Our path to finding each other was a maze. It was truly a miracle that we had found each other. In his email to me, my then possible half-brother wrote that he was given up for adoption after he was born in Colorado. His adoptive parents lived in California and had never told him that he was adopted. He did not learn this until long after his adoptive mother and father had died.

He explained that his wife had been going through an old scrapbook kept by his adoptive mother. There she found a draft of a letter written by his adoptive mother to his adoptive father's great aunt who ran a maternity hospital. The letter asked the aunt if she could assist a friend of the adoptive parents with adoption the way the great aunt had assisted them with their adoption. From this, he realized that he had been adopted and his adoptive father's great aunt had arranged and facilitated his adoption. This came as a great shock and surprise.

Getting up the courage, he wrote to the aunt who was then over 90 years old. Fortunately, she had kept the birth and adoption documents for him for all of those years in case he ever came looking for them. They were sent immediately and his journey to discover his biological family began. He had met his biological mother and his half-sister and half-brother many years before we began our explorations. Prior to DNA testing, he wrote that he did not know that there would be more family still.

My possible half-brother was certain that my dad had never even known about him. I asked him if he would mind taking another DNA test with another company where I had already tested. He did so. While waiting for the results, we got to know each other. I was sure that this man was my half-brother. I had Dad's navy picture, and I had found my half-brother's high school picture through Google. If you covered the faces and looked at the eyes, they were so much the same. Amazing what you can find online!

On the day my half-brother's 2nd DNA testing results came in, he texted and said, "You are my half-sister, Susan. Why don't we celebrate and actually talk to each other on the phone?" We talked for about five hours that first day.

I did not tell anyone about my new half-brother until after my mom passed away. If she had found out 20 years before this, she would have welcomed Dad's son with open arms. However, in the days at the end of her life, I was afraid that she would get confused and think that perhaps Dad had cheated on her. I was protecting her. My half-sibling was happy to go along with anything I thought was right. He is a very kind man.

A year after all this unfolded, David and I made the trip before the Covid 19 pandemic in 2020 to visit him and his wife in California. I gasped as they walked into the lobby of our hotel. I could hardly look him in the eyes. I was looking into my dad's eyes.

He smiled. There was Dad's cheek dimple. We hugged tightly. I looked at David through my tears, and there were tears in his eyes. Tears of joy! We talked and talked for two days and began a great relationship. God has brought this dear man and his wife into our lives as a blessing. We text back and forth every week or call or FaceTime. I find that I can talk to him about anything. I feel peaceful in talking with him. He is a fine man, and I am proud to call him my brother.

When I think that I began this journey because I had no children born to my body and thought I could look back to my ancestors, I have an amazing thought. If I had not had the hysterectomy and had a child of my own, would I have thought to join Ancestry and look back? If I had not joined Ancestry, I never would have found my half-brother. God does work all things, as hard as they may be, for good to those who love Him. The song on my heart today rings so true, *Now Thank We All Our God.*

> *Now thank we all our God with hearts and hands and voices.*
> *Who wondrous things has done, in whom His world rejoices.*
> *Who from our mother's arms, has blessed us on our way with*
> *countless gifts of love, and still is ours today.*[55]

~~~~~~~~~~~~~~~~~~~~~~~~~~~~~~~~~~~~~~~

LET'S TALK ABOUT GOD'S GOODNESS:

This experience of finding a new half-brother was a big shock in my life. It threw me off balance just when I thought I had everything family-wise figured out in my life. I had been researching to find my ancestors, not a sibling. It was scary at times. It was totally unexpected. I didn't know whom to tell and decided to keep it to myself because of concern for my mother and the confusion it might bring her.

---

[55] Rinkart, Martin, Copyright © 1636, "Nun danket alle Gott", Catherine Winkworth translated it from German to "Now Thank We All Our God", in the Public Domain.

It was also a very confusing time for me. However, God in his goodness had brought about this meeting. It was good for my half-brother to have some closure on who his father was. It was amazing to get to know a complete stranger who is related by DNA and is my actual brother. We have many similarities but also differences as would any siblings. My brother has now communicated with his new half-brother, and they are getting to know each other. Wonder of wonders! This was a great gift of goodness from the Lord.

For me, finding my new half-brother was so refreshing in my life. You already know that I believe God is in control even in the most terrible situations. I believe that when you accept Jesus as Lord and the Holy Spirit dwells in you, He will guide you through tough times and good times and help you find joy. He is faithful to bring you peace, hope, and sometimes unexpected gifts. In the Bible:

> Because of the Lord's great love, we are not consumed, for His compassions never fail. They are new every morning; great is Your faithfulness.
>
> **Lamentations 3:22-23 (NIV)**

KEY TO FINDING GOD'S JOY #25:

When living a life close to God, expect the unexpected. This is a God of surprises! You never know what life and God have that will be coming into your life. Through His love for us, He shares His goodness and joy.

PRAYERFULLY THINK ABOUT YOUR OWN LIFE WITH GOD:

I wonder if you have experienced finding a new blessing in your life when all seems bleak. Perhaps you, also, have found a new half-sibling or relative you didn't know about in the past. Maybe it was a good experience, or I have heard from some that it was an experience of rejection. It is hard to be a human. We don't know what is coming at us next. It could be that you haven't had this type of surprise in your life, but has God brought other surprises to you that you didn't expect? You may have had a new job fall in your lap, or perhaps you have lost a job. Maybe you needed to move unexpectantly. You may have found a new friend who has been God's greatest blessing to you.

All of these surprises of life can feel uncomfortable at first. If you are depending on God, He can show you his goodness through them. The goodness may not show right away. It may take a while to figure out what God is doing in your life. But once again, God is in control. Have you had the unexpected pop up? How did it affect you? Did you find God's goodness in it yet, or are you struggling with the change in your life? Take a few moments to reflect on your surprises in life and how they have affected you.

_____

_____

_____

_____

_____

_____

_____

_____

_____

_____

A Song of God's Love and Purpose for Your Life

Oh for the wonderful love He has promised,
promised for you and for me!
- William Lamartine Thompson

"Susan," Mom said. "I finally know why God still has me here on earth."

"Why Mom? You've been here in the nursing home now for a year. I know you've wanted to go see Jesus for all of that time, but what have you learned?"

"It's Tycka."

"Tycka?" I had no idea where Mom was going with this realization.

"You know how Tycka has taken me under her wing at dinner lately. The aides take me down to the 2nd floor for dinner where more people talk. We have good conversations, and she always saves a place for me. Yesterday she said she could tell I was at peace about my pain and about dying. She asked how I did that. I told her I depend on my faith in Jesus to give me peace in my life no matter where I am or how long I live. She very proudly told me she was an atheist. She wasn't into that religion thing. She said we would agree to disagree."

Later at dinners, Mom would hear her talk about her atheism. She was very proud of it and wanted everyone to know about it. The nurses, the aides, and the residents all knew that Tycka was an atheist. Tycka made sure that was so.

The Holy Spirit was working in Mom's heart now. Mom made a point of not pushing or bringing up the subject of Jesus to Tycka but just loving her as her friend. However, Tycka brought it up many times in the next months. Sometimes Mom didn't make it down to the 2nd floor for dinner. Tycka who was 100 years old made a point of using her walker and making it down the long hall to the elevator to Mom's 3rd floor. She would then walk the long distance to Mom's room to see how she was doing. Again, Tycka would bring up Jesus, they would talk a while, and then Tycka would say they would agree to disagree.

The last time I saw Tycka, I pushed Mom in her wheelchair down to the 2nd floor to visit her. "Oh, Cecile and Susan! I'm so glad to see you. I think I'm on my last legs now. I'm very weak. I just have to tell you about something very strange that happened last night. My subconscious started going through my life and telling me all the things I had done wrong, and I repented." Usually, I just sat and listened to their conversation. This time I spoke. "Tycka. That wasn't your subconscious. That was God and the Holy Spirit speaking to you."

Mom asked her if she wanted to pray with her. Tycka declined. Then Mom said, "Tycka, if you ever feel the Lord leading you to want to pray to Him, to ask forgiveness for your sins, and to accept Jesus into your heart, all you have to do is have one of the nurses send an aide to get me. I will come and pray with you."

"I don't think so. We will agree to disagree, Cecile. You know I have always been an atheist."

I spoke up again, fearful that this dear woman who loved my mom would die alone and never know Jesus in her heart. "Tycka, you know if you feel yourself slipping away, all you have to do is say I believe and then reach out and take Jesus' hand." She smiled, and we left.

The week before Tycka died at 101 years old, she asked the nurse to send an aide to get my mom. The aide asked Mom, "Are you really going to pray with Tycka? Isn't she an atheist?" Then the girl said, "I've never been to church. Do you think it's too late for me?" Mom assured her that it wasn't and that she should come back sometime and they could talk.

When Mom arrived at Tycka's room, she was weak but she said, "Cecile. I want to pray to God and ask Him to be with me and forgive me for my sins." Mom led her through the prayer, and Tycka cried. Her heart had received Jesus as her Lord and Savior. She had the peace that passes all understanding. Ah! God's call in love is in the hymn, *Softly and Tenderly Jesus Is Calling*.

> *Softly and tenderly Jesus is calling, calling for you and for me;*
> *see on the portals He's waiting and watching, watching for you and for me.*
> *Come home, come home, ye who are weary come home;*
> *earnestly tenderly Jesus is calling, calling O sinner come home.*[56]

---

[56] Thompson, William Lamartine, Copyright © 1880, "Softly and Tenderly Jesus Is Calling", Words and Music in the Public Domain.

God was calling Tycka, but He had also called Mom to listen and obey.

The next week, Mom's nurse, Liz, asked if she wanted to go down to say goodbye to Tycka. She was now in a coma, but Mom could have a final time with her. Entering her room, Liz pushed Mom's wheelchair right next to Tycka's bed.

Liz described the time this way. "Your mom took Tycka's hand. It was like the Holy Spirit just went through your mom's hand into Tycka's heart. She had been in a coma all day, but she opened her eyes, looked at your mom, and smiled the sweetest smile I have ever seen on anyone's face. Your mom prayed over her, and Tycka went back into her coma stage."

The next morning, a woman came running down Mom's hallway while Mom was at breakfast. "Where's my angel?" she was asking. Liz pointed out Mom. Sue, Tycka's daughter-in-law, was in a Bible study, and they had been praying for Tycka for years and years. The family all knew she was an atheist. God had brought Mom into Tycka's life to answer those many years of prayers. A few days before the coma, they had realized a difference in Tycka, and their mom had relayed that she had accepted that God and Jesus were real. She had asked forgiveness for her sins. Tycka had peace! All Sue could say to Mom was, "Thank you for leading my mother-in-law to the Lord before she dies. What a blessing you have been in her life and all of our lives. Thank you!" Tycka went to Heaven the next day.

After being in the nursing home for a year, my mom had wondered why Jesus still had her here on earth. She listened to God, and he told her "Tycka". God's purpose had been fulfilled miraculously. A devout atheist had come to know Jesus as her personal Savior and Lord.

At the time, Mom was at the end stages of her life. She was almost 95 and struggling with her health. And yet, God still had a plan and a purpose for Mom's life. He loved Tycka so much that he brought Mom this awareness of her purpose. At 94 years of age, God was not done writing Mom's story.

~~~~~~~~~~~~~~~~~~~~~~~~~~~~

LET'S TALK ABOUT GOD'S LOVE AND PURPOSE FOR YOUR LIFE:

A great tragedy in a Christian's life would be not having a purpose. God sees the best in you and has a purpose for you. Huntley Brown, a famous pianist who has played for the Billy Graham Association and at Billy Graham's funeral, recently played and preached at our church. He told the story of Gideon who was the least likely to be called by God to be a great warrior for God. Gideon was called to help free the Israelites from the hands of the Midianites. He couldn't even believe what God was telling him:

> "Pardon me, my Lord", Gideon replied, "but how can I save Israel? My clan is the weakest in Manasseh, and I am the least in my family."
> The Lord answered, "I will be with you..."
> **Judges 6:15-16 (NIV)**

Gideon listened and accomplished God's mission for him. God is with all of us when we are called to His purpose.

Our lesson in all of this should be that God has a purpose for those who love Him, because He loves all people in the world. He will be with us. We can be His instruments to bring God's love to others.

A friend of mine from college, Jay Newman, is the administrator of a private but open to others group on Facebook called "Positivity Power". A recent post by Jay about God's love touched my heart. I asked Jay for permission to print it here.

"If God had preconditions to being eligible to receive the love felt for us, Jesus would never have been born! If God set the same preconditions that we set for each other, we wouldn't have a prayer. Face it, we would be doomed! Whether God loves us isn't even the question! How much God loves is not the question either! The only question that we each need to answer is, 'How much do I love God?' I know that ability to love is limitless! But, I also know that being able to is not the same as doing! If I love God as much as I say I do, my marching orders will always be: 'Who would Jesus love?' and 'How would He show that love?'"

How do we find God's love for others and His purpose in our lives? First, listen to God. How do we listen? First, we read His Word in the Bible. New insights come to us all the time through reading or rereading scripture. Try to not just take bits and pieces but see them in the context of the whole Bible and the time and culture in which it was written. In other words, study it.

Attend church and Bible study to learn all you can about the Lord. Make sure your pastor is a man who also listens to God's word and will in his life and is a humble man. Listen carefully to your pastor's sermons. Through this learning, God's purpose may emerge for you.

Second, listen to God by praying and then being still to allow God to touch your soul. God can speak to your heart. Have you not heard that voice in your heart saying, *"You really shouldn't do that. Are you really going to walk by that person in need? How about if you invite that person to church? Why don't you introduce yourself to that person? You need to forgive that person. That person needs someone to pay for their groceries. What about that neighbor? Don't you think you should be praying for them? I know you don't like being around that person, but I have my purpose in having you there. That friend of yours who never does anything for you... needs you. I love you!"* Listen to that voice and act.

Finally, we can ask God through prayer what exactly He wants us to do. Perhaps God has a specific purpose for you that you would not discover without asking. My mom was constantly asking, "God. Why do you still have me here? I am ready to come to see you." God answered her question. *Tycka!*

KEY TO FINDING GOD'S JOY #26:

Why are you here on earth? Our God gives each of us purpose in life. He is also loving and patient. If we are His disciples, God brings people into our lives and we can love them and care for them. We can also help them to know the love of Jesus deeply in their hearts. This happens at just the right time when they are ready to hear God's voice through the Holy Spirit. Perhaps our purpose is to simply plant a seed of God's power and love in someone's heart. At other times, it is our opportunity to be there when God brings true awareness of His amazing grace and love into their hearts. What joy we find when another finds true peace in the Lord Jesus Christ!

In Tycka's case, God loved her and was patient for 101 years. I'm sure over the years He used her daughter-in-law and many others or situations to plant seeds in her heart. And then, He brought His person (my mom) into Tycka's life to help Him bring about a complete change, repentance, and joy to her heart before she died. What a miracle it is every time someone's life is changed so completely. The angels rejoice and sing! How amazing is that joy and peace that passes all understanding!

PRAYERFULLY THINK ABOUT YOUR OWN LIFE WITH GOD:

God is patient in His love for us. He teaches us through His word and helps us to find His purpose for us, especially when we ask Him to do so. These opportunities are there for us during our entire lives. Whether at 15 or 95 years old, God can still give you His purpose in this life. Through studying His word, listening to His voice with our hearts, learning from other Christians, and asking Him for our purpose, we begin to become all that He wants us to be in this life before we meet Him in Heaven.

Have you asked God what His purpose is in your life? Have you spent time getting to know God through His word and through prayers? Have you appreciated God's patience with you as you learn slowly? Would someone see something different in you - something that only God can give you through His grace and the Holy Spirit? If not, what will you do about that? Has God ever used you to touch someone else's life through helping them or showing them the love of Jesus? What happened? Take some time to reflect on what God has done already in your life. If this hasn't been a part of your experience, what could God have in store for you and how might you get there for others?

A Song of God's Worthiness of Awe, Fear, and Praise

To God all glory, praise, and love
be now and ever given
by saints below and saints above,
the Church in earth and heaven.
- Charles Wesley

*C*hange! I have always said how I dislike it. But I also know that without change, we don't grow in the Lord. Right now, the church which David and I attend is experiencing change. The same is happening with churches everywhere. We had the experience of going through not meeting as a congregation because of the Covid 19 pandemic of 2020-2021, and instead, we tried zooming on computers. It was actually against the law to gather in groups, and we wore masks everywhere. When we came back together, there were still the mask mandates and new rules to follow. At a church dinner, only one person with gloves could touch the serving spoon, so we went through a type of cafeteria line. Weddings or funerals were postponed since interstate travel or overseas travel was banned.

Many people did not return quickly to church when some conditions were lifted, due to fear, perhaps due to rebellion against the new rules, or just maybe it was very nice to stay home on Sunday mornings to watch the church service in their pajamas or not even watch. If the latter reasons were true, it makes me very sad for the church. We know the church is a body of believers, not the actual building. So, however things change with how people are members of the church body, I cannot sit in judgment. I am never allowed to sit in judgment. I am commanded to love. It just makes me sad not to see them and share the experience of worshipping God with the whole body of believers who attend our church.

Another change with our church is that we have been in the middle of a change of pastors. Our transitional pastor was wonderful, and we all felt close to him and encouraged and taught by his words for us on Sunday morning. However, he was called to pursue a different ministry once we officially launched our search for our new pastor. My dear friend, Andy, is now filling the need for teaching on Sundays while we wait for our new pastor. What a gift he has been to our congregation.

We are in the midst of trying to find the pastor who will be a dedicated humble follower of God, who knows the Bible, and who has messages of meaning and teaching for us each week. We need to be challenged to depend on God in all circumstances. We also need a shepherd who can lead our leaders and meet the emotional and spiritual needs of our church community. Our church is a family. We love and help one another. I am so thankful for all of my friends at Westminster Presbyterian Church. We are also hopeful to find a pastor with a vision to show love to our whole community. God is love.

We as a church have been encouraged to meet together to "hash out" the mission of our church, especially in the present age. Should many ways of doing things change? How can we best show love to others who may come to our church or do not come to church at all? Remember, knowing Jesus is about relationship, not the church building and rituals. In the last meeting we had, I did a lot of thinking about our direction and the hearts of all in our congregation and of the church in general in the world. My mind kept going to the fear of the Lord in our members. Also, praise to our God is key to having our hearts and minds in the place to receive all God wants for our church. The song in my mind?

> *O for a thousand tongues to sing, my great Redeemer's praise. The glories of my God and King, the triumphs of His grace. My gracious Master and my God assist me to proclaim; To spread thru all the earth abroad, the honors of Thy name.*[57]

David and I are praying that God will use all of us at church and our new minister yet to come to show the love of our awesome God to all. We give Him all praise!

~~~~~~~~~~~~~~~~~~~~~~~~~~~~

LET'S TALK ABOUT GOD'S WORTHINESS OF AWE, FEAR, AND PRAISE:

Our church is in transition, but all churches should be thinking of how God is shown His rightful place in our midst. My heart knows that we need to make sure that God is also in His rightful place in our own lives. If you are not filled with the fear of God, and by that, I mean a Holy Reverential Awe of God, it is very difficult for you to be His instrument in helping others. What is the fear of the Lord?

> The fear of the Lord is the beginning of knowledge, but fools despise wisdom and instruction.
>
> **Proverbs 1:7 (NIV)**

---

[57] Wesley, Charles, Copyright © 1739, "O For A Thousand Tongues to Sing My Dear Redeemer's Praise", in the Public Domain.

The fear of the Lord is the beginning of wisdom; all who follow His precepts have good understanding. To Him belongs eternal praise.

Psalm 111:10 (NIV)

The fear of the Lord leads to life; then one rests content, untouched by trouble.

Proverbs 19:23 (NIV)

Therefore God exalted Him to the highest place and gave Him the name that is above every name, that at the name of Jesus every knee should bow, in heaven and on earth and under the_earth, and every tongue acknowledge that Jesus Christ is Lord, to the glory of God the Father. Therefore, my dear friends, as you have always obeyed - not only in my presence, but now much more in my absence - continue to work out your salvation with fear and trembling, for it is God who worksin you to will and to act in order to fulfill His good purpose.

Philippians 2:9-13 (NIV)

I am just wondering if we have thought enough about the fear of the Lord. It is part of the Spirit of the Lord in us. It seems through these verses from the Bible that without the fear of the Lord, we will not have the beginnings of knowledge and understanding, wisdom and insight, and maybe even salvation for some. Without praise and the awe of the Lord, I myself will be on the throne of my life, but I don't have the power and the love on my own. I am an imperfect being. Only through the Holy Spirit working through me, do I find love for all including the unlovable. I also find the power to ask for forgiveness and to forgive, the wisdom to know God's path for me, and the courage to do what God wants, even if it puts me in danger.

I need the awe of the Lord in my heart to find joy and work out God's purpose in my life.

KEY TO FINDING GOD'S JOY #27:

Make sure that God is seated in His rightful place on the throne of your life. He is worthy to be praised. Find the fear of the Lord in your heart to gain knowledge, wisdom, and discernment about life. This will bring you joy in all times of life for you will be in awe!

PRAYERFULLY THINK ABOUT YOUR OWN LIFE WITH GOD:

If we have become part of God's kingdom, He is faithful to offer us opportunities to grow in awe, wisdom, and knowledge. His love for us makes our way straight when it has been crooked. We are all in different places in our relationships with God. Do you have a fear of the Lord that gives you His knowledge, wisdom, and guidance in life?

Think of a time when you were in awe of some wisdom you came upon in God's word or by listening to Him. What was that wisdom you learned? When was the last time God made your way straight instead of crooked? How did it change your life? If you are most important and on the throne of your life, have you realized that you don't have the power to make true changes? God is in control. If you realize that God is not on the throne of your life, what can you do about that? What changes do you need to make to find the full joy that praising our awesome God can bring? Some more questions to ponder.

A Song of
God's Trustworthiness

'Tis so sweet to trust in Jesus,
Just to take
Him at his word,
Just to rest upon His promise,
Just to know "Thus saith the Lord".
- Louisa M.R. Stead and William J. Fitzpatrick

"You still have a chance of getting more blood clots," my doctor said. "One of your blood markers is high after you took your six months of blood thinners. You may even have another autoimmune disease which could cause clots in any organ at any moment. We'll keep track of this with a blood test over time."

"This is not good," I said. There it was again. Worry! Fear! My human response to the unknown. When will I learn? It takes a lifetime with Jesus.

"Don't worry. We will keep track of your markers. They could go down."

I felt that fear that God does not want us to have when facing problems. He wants us to trust in Him and to give us His peace.

... I do believe; help me overcome my unbelief.

Mark 9:24 (NIV)

At home that night, I sat at the computer looking up websites about the high markers. David looked over my shoulder. "Susan, will immersing yourself in this help you? You're going 'down the rabbit hole' looking for information again. Why don't we pray about this?"

My wise husband, David!!

"Lord, God. Almighty Healer. I pray for peace in the waiting for new tests. Help me to hand this over to you and not ruin each new day You give me with worry. I do believe that You are in control. Thank You, Lord!"

After prayer, God has truly given me the peace to wait on future results. What would I do without my Lord? I have joy that I can place my life completely in God's hands, lean into Him, and trust that He is in control. I am grateful!

The hymn which has me singing today is *'Tis So Sweet to Trust in Jesus*.

> *Yes 'tis sweet to trust in Jesus; just from sin and self to cease. Just from Jesus simply taking, life and rest and joy and peace. Jesus Jesus, how I trust Him. How I've proved Him o'er and o'er. Jesus Jesus, precious Jesus; O for grace to trust Him more. I'm so glad I learned to trust Thee, Precious Jesus Savior Friend. And I know that Thou art with me; wilt be with me to the end.*[58]

What a promise!

~~~~~~~~~~~~~~~~~~~~~~~~~~~~~~~~~~

LET'S TALK ABOUT GOD'S TRUSTWORTHINESS:

When we first become Christians, we haven't had many experiences of putting our trust in God. It is harder to do this. We have learned from God's Spirit for a short period and have not had enough time to see how the Lord is faithful to be with us throughout our walk with Him. Trust in the Lord comes to us more and more as we are

---

[58] Stead, Louisa M. R. (words), William J. Kirkpatrick (music), Copyright © 1882, "'Tis So Sweet To Trust In Jesus", *Songs of Triumph,* in the Public Domain.

transformed by the Holy Spirit. Yet, my immediate reaction to this situation had been fear. God is constantly teaching me and assuring me as I travel through life with Him.

On April 15, 2022, Barb called me to wish me a happy 50th Spiritual Birthday. We accepted Jesus completely into our hearts fifty years ago in that café in Rock Island, and the Holy Spirit still is teaching me. The difference is that now I say, "Of course. God is with me straightening my path. Thank You, Lord!"

Paul wrote to the Romans in the Bible, and this is my hope for us all:

> May the God of all hope fill you with all joy and peace as you trust in Him, so that you may overflow with hope by the power of the Holy Spirit.
>
> **Romans 15:13 (NIV)**

As we realize God's trustworthiness in being with us every moment of our lives during the good and the bad times, we can relax in Him. Turning our thoughts to the service of others at these times can take our focus from a problem to the wonder-working power of God.

In a booklet called *I Will Trust God: Meditations For Recovery From Loss and Grief* by Paul F. Keller, Day Fifty-Seven points us in the right direction - "There is nothing you can do about the past, but something you can do about this day. Again, the emphasis is on the path of love and service simply because when you are doing works of love in service of others, you are healing and recovering. And what you do lives on in others; what you do as acts of love and service today never really die because love and service continue to infect others, and thus your simple offerings become a joy from age to age."[59]

KEY TO FINDING GOD'S JOY #28:

Trust in Jesus, and you will be filled with gratitude as He teaches you and helps you grow in your faith. This will allow you to have joy no matter what your circumstances. It is a spiritual joy. Live each day as if it is your last, loving God and other people.

PRAYERFULLY THINK ABOUT YOUR OWN LIFE WITH GOD:

Do you have a fear right now that is always on your mind? It could be about you, another person, or something in the world. What is that fear? If you are a newer Christian, you may not have seen yet how trustworthy God can be. Even if your worst fear comes true, He will be with you to hold you fast. You can lean on Him. Are you worried about war or food shortage or illness? God doesn't want you to worry. What can you do to trust Him with these problems? If Jesus is whom he said He was, you can trust him! Take a few moments to reflect on the trustworthiness of God and how it relates to your life.

---

[59] Keller, Paul F., Copyright © 1984, *I Will Trust God: Meditations for Recovery from Loss and Grief*, Minneapolis, Minnesota: Kairos No. 8480, Extracted from Day Fifty-Seven. All rights reserved. Used by permission.

Conclusion:
A Final Song

*The love of God is greater far
than tongue or pen can ever tell.*
*- Fredrick Martin Lehman and
Claudia Lehman Mays*

$\mathcal{Y}$ou may have said to yourself as you have read through this devotional journey, *"I don't know. My troubles are greater than these. How can I stop having doubt and fear? Can I give this all to God? Is He truly there to help me through all the trials of life? Will He give me joy in my soul?"* Let's look at our journey.

We have learned that God's song in your soul includes His nurturing, patience, and true grace of forgiveness and salvation from your sins. He offers you gifts of the Spirit.

God provides guidance in your life and true joy deep in your heart. He offers provisions for you and restoration in many different circumstances. He models for His children how to get through life and gives them the strength to get through tough times.

The Lord blesses you and cares for you beyond all measure. Sometimes it is with that which you don't even notice, and sometimes it is through a difficult time in your life. He has strong arms to carry you through those tough times.

God is awesome and powerful in His assurance and in the beauty of the earth.. so worthy to be praised.

In your troubles in life, He gives you his refuge and hope that you will find your way through the darkness to his light, and He encourages you in many ways. Many times He blesses you with great gifts.

God gives you peace in your losses and helps you find acceptance of the reality that the loss has happened even though your loss will still be felt.

God provides protection and amazes you with His creation of you and all around you. God's presence is there whether He brings you through with miracles or you depend on Him through faith when He doesn't feel near. He is there! He is in control.

God's goodness can bring new people or new interests into your life. He blesses you in life's changes. God loves you more than you can even realize, and no matter your age, He has a purpose for you in the Kingdom of God.

All these character traits of God are the reason we can have full trust in Him. Hallelujah! In the Bible, Paul describes living as a Christian:

> Therefore, as God's chosen people, holy and dearly loved, clothe yourselves with compassion, kindness, humility, gentleness, and patience. Bear with each other and forgive one another if any of you has a grievance against someone. Forgive as the Lord forgave you. And

over all these virtues put on love, which binds them all together in perfect unity.

Let the peace of Christ rule in your hearts, since as members of one body you were called to peace. And be thankful. Let the message of Christ dwell among you richly as you teach and admonish one another with all wisdom through psalms, hymns, and songs from the Spirit, singing to God with gratitude in your hearts. And whatever you do, whether in word or deed, do it all in the name of the Lord Jesus, giving thanks to God the Father through Him.

Colossians 3:12-17 (NIV)

All of our blessings and deep down joy come to us through God. It is a joy so deep that it is hard to even express, and it is the knowledge that it is there no matter what our circumstances. We can have <u>faith</u> in a God we cannot see but Who is there! And when we <u>hope</u> and trust, it is the sweetest feeling in our souls. We will be grateful and at peace!

Salvation through Jesus is not only about going to heaven. It is about living in the Lord's kingdom here on earth as part of His family. When we accept that Jesus is here for us, He sends his Holy Spirit to dwell in our hearts. It is the presence of the Holy Spirit within our souls that teaches, prays, comforts, and transforms us. The Spirit sheds light on Jesus. We learn and have the beginnings of an understanding of all of Jesus' teachings. Jesus taught us to <u>love</u> God and others as ourselves. He taught us to look out for the needs of the poor. He taught us by his example of whom He came to befriend in His journey here on earth (the lowly and the sinful) before His final task of dying for our sins.

Oh, the great love of Jesus! My final song was difficult to choose. My sentimental side chose my Grandma's favorite hymn, *The Love of God.*

> *Verse 3: Could we with ink the ocean fill and were the skies of parchment made; Were every stalk on earth a quill, and every man a scribe by trade; To write the love of God above would drain the ocean dry; Nor could the scroll contain the whole though stretched from sky to sky.*
> *Chorus: O love of God, how rich and pure; how measureless and strong. It shall forevermore endure, the saints and angels' song.*[60]

In no way could I completely communicate the love of God through my words in this book. It is far greater than we can imagine. You will find it in your journey when you depend on God.

God will give you love for others that can be seen by them. That love will show itself in your care for their needs, your prayers for them, and your desire for them to find God's best path. What a blessing it is when others ask you how you get through the tough times, because they see peace and joy in your heart and the Holy Spirit in your eyes. Through your love for others, God lets them see something different in you that they need - a relationship with the Lord Jesus Christ who will present them to His Father cleansed from their sins. They will also find life here on earth to be full of God's presence, glory, peace, love, and joy. They will find God's song in their souls! While you, through God, are doing this for others in your

---

[60] Lehman, Frederick M. (words) and Claudia Lehman Mays (music), Copyright © 1917, "The Love of God", in the Public Domain.

painful or fantastic times of life, you too will find God's song in your soul! God is so good.

> And now these three remain: faith, hope, and love.
> But the greatest of these is love.
> **1st Corinthians 13:13 (NIV)**

> The Lord is my strength and my shield; my heart trusts in Him, and He helps me. My heart leaps for joy, and with my song I praise Him.
> **Psalm 28:7 (NIV)**

In your love for God, in His love for you, and in your difficulties, you will find true joy!!

A FINAL LOOK AT YOUR OWN LIFE WITH GOD:

Do you realize that being a Christian is not about following rules, going to church, and doing all those rituals or activities which have been such a part of the Christian religion? Much of that is all good in God's eyes, but do you understand that knowing God is not a religion? It is a relationship with the God of the Universe. Just today in church, Andy talked about a pastor who had been Presbyterian all of his life. Many were surprised when the Lord worked in this man's life so strongly that he was telling everyone he had newly become a Christian. Although he had worked in God's service and seemed like a Christian to all who knew him, God had come in and changed his life. He knew he was different. His focus was now as a follower of Jesus in all directions in his life. He had become a new Christian. When you give your heart to God, do you know the Holy Spirit is within you and transforming you as you experience your relationship with God? The transformation will bring you even closer to His example for us. Have you thought about how much

God loves you? The Lord is worthy to be trusted and praised. Reflect on our entire journey together. Write a few thoughts here about your <u>true</u> relationship with God - the Father, His son the Lord Jesus Christ, and the Holy Spirit. What is it that you still need to do to know God and His joy deep in your heart? I will be praying for you. God bless you in a mighty way and give you peace, gratitude, and His joy - God's song in your soul!

_____

_____

_____

_____

_____

_____

_____

_____

_____

_____

_____

_____

_____

_____

_____

_____

About the Author

This book came about by Susan Berg Heeg's constant desire to know our Creator in a deeper more personal way. After becoming a Christian, music has been a very important part of her life. She has sung in church choirs and loves to sing along with hymns in the car as she drives. Having had many ups and downs in life, Susan has shared many of the lessons of her spiritual journey to find joy amidst pain, difficulty, and good times too, with churches, Christian groups, and on television.

Married to the most wonderful man, David Heeg, life has been a blessing. Susan also has two stepsons, David Jr. with his wife, Andrea, and Jason Sr. with his wife, Mish. She is also blessed with six grandchildren who have brought her a bounty of laughs and hugs and love... Kathryn, David III, Andrew, Jason Jr., Anthony, and Emma.

Susan dedicated herself for 34 years to children as a teacher of 3rd graders, children with learning disabilities, or children with behavior disorders. She is now retired from the career she loved. As an author and member of the Society for Children's Book Writers and Illustrators, Susan was honored by the Illinois Reading Association at a luncheon for Illinois authors.

Susan Berg Heeg's first book, *Voyage to Victory: The Voice of a Sailor in the Pacific 1943-1945,* grew from a collection of letters her dad wrote to the members of his family during World War II. While researching for her book, she collected many WWII artifacts. A Jan./Feb.1943 *Superman* comic book with Superman helping the U.S. Navy in the Pacific began her collection. The letters and her artifacts led to presentations for schools, churches, veteran's groups, libraries, senior living facilities, and conferences. This book and research also led Susan to think of the fear and experiences her dad and other servicemen and women in war must survive with the reality of death all around them. Those thoughts began her exploration of how her dad found his way with his faith in God to get through the war. It also brought her to see God's work in her own life of difficulties. Thus, this second book was born.

Susan's greatest desire is that all will find God's song in their souls and the joy and peace that only God can give even in the most difficult situations of life. For information on book talks about Susan Berg Heeg's newest book, *God's Song in Your Soul: Keys to Finding Joy in the Midst of Difficulties – A Devotional Journey*, see the contact information below.

Contact Information for Susan Berg Heeg:

Website - susanbergheeg.com

Facebook - Susan Berg Heeg

SusanBergHeegAuthor@gmail.com

Susan's grandchildren posed with the family after their last marionette show!
Front: Mish, David III, Anthony, Emma, Jake, and Andrew
Back: Jason, David Sr., Susan, Susan's Mom, Kathryn, Andrea, and David Jr.

Made in the USA
Coppell, TX
20 October 2022

85009399R00134